Cambridge Primary

Hodder Cambridge Primary
Maths

Learner's Book

LEMONADE

Sale!
25% free

Stage 5

Steph King

Series editors: Mike Askew
and Paul Broadbent

HODDER
EDUCATION
AN HACHETTE UK COMPANY

Author acknowledgements

With warm thanks to Jennifer Peek for her help in shaping and developing this title.

The Publisher is extremely grateful to the following schools for their comments and feedback during the development of this series:

Avalon Heights World Private School, Ajman

The Oxford School, Dubai

Al Amana Private School, Sharjah

British International School, Ajman

Wesgreen International School, Sharjah

As Seeb International School, Al Khoud.

Photograph acknowledgements

We would like to thank the following for their permission to reproduce photographs:

p.28 t © Poemsuk Kinchokawat/123rf; **p.28** b © Olga Bosnak/123rf; **p.30** © Welcomia/123rf; **p.34** © Dmytro Demianenko/123rf; **p.46** © Ruslan Nassyrov/123rf; **p.53** © Moodboard/Alamy Stock Photo; **p.56** © 400_Tmax/Getty Images; **p.59** © ASB63/123rf; **p.67** © Andriy Popov/123rf; **p.88**, **p.165** © Hachette UK; **p.90** © Granger Historical Picture Archive/Alamy Stock Photo; **p.107** © Russell Hart/Alamy Stock Photo; **p.114** © S Jenner13/123rf; **p.148** © Geoff Williamson Selected/Alamy Stock Photo; **p.157** © Eugene Sergeev/123rf; **p.168** © Chris Hill/Shutterstock.

t = top, b = bottom, l = left, r = right, c = centre

Practise test exam-style questions and sample answers are written by the author.

Every effort has been made to trace all copyright holders, but if any have been inadvertently overlooked the Publishers will be pleased to make the necessary arrangements at the first opportunity.

Although every effort has been made to ensure that website addresses are correct at time of going to press, Hodder Education cannot be held responsible for the content of any website mentioned in this book. It is sometimes possible to find a relocated web page by typing in the address of the home page for a website in the URL window of your browser.

Hachette UK's policy is to use papers that are natural, renewable and recyclable products and made from wood grown in sustainable forests. The logging and manufacturing processes are expected to conform to the environmental regulations of the country of origin.

Orders: please contact Hachette UK Distribution, Hely Hutchinson Centre, Milton Road, Didcot, Oxfordshire, OX11 7HH. Telephone: +44 (0)1235 827827. Email education@hachette.co.uk Lines are open from 9 a.m. to 5 p.m., Monday to Friday. You can also order through our website: www.hoddereducation.com

Cover illustration Steven Evans

Illustrations by Alex van Howelingen and DTP Impressions

Typeset in FS Albert 12/14 by DTP Impressions

Printed by CPI Group (UK) Ltd, Croydon CR0 4YY

A catalogue record for this title is available from the British Library

9781471884405

Contents

Introduction 5

Term 1

Unit 1 Number and problem solving 6
1a Place value and the number system 6
1b Rounding and estimating 11
1c Addition and subtraction 14

Unit 2 Measures and problem solving 21
2a The metric system 21
2b Length, area and perimeter 23
2c Time 28
2d Problem solving 31

Unit 3 Number and problem solving 34
3a Number patterns 34
3b Multiplication and division 38
3c Problem solving 46

Unit 4 Geometry and problem solving 49
4a Classifying 2-D shapes 49
4b 3-D and 2-D shapes 51
4c Working with coordinates 54
4d Transformations 56
4e Problem solving 59

Unit 5 Problem solving and review 63
5a Problem solving 63

Term 2

Unit 6 Number and problem solving 67
6a Place value and the number system 67
6b Rounding and ordering 70
6c Addition and subtraction 75

Unit 7 Measures and problem solving 83
7a The metric system 83
7b Length, area and perimeter 86
7c Time 88
7d Problem solving 90

Unit 8 Number and problem solving 93
8a Number patterns 93
8b Multiplication and division 96

Unit 9 Handling data and problem solving 107
9a Organising, categorising and representing data 107
9b Probability 111
9c Problem solving 114

Unit 10 Problem solving and review 118
10a Problem solving 118

I am Afia.

Term 3

Unit 11 Number and problem solving   **122**

11a   Rounding and ordering   122
11b   Fractions   127
11c   Addition and subtraction   133

Unit 12 Measures and problem solving   **137**

12a   The metric system   137
12b   Length, area and perimeter   140
12c   Time   142

Unit 13 Number and problem solving   **146**

13a   Number patterns   146
13b   Multiplication and division   148

Unit 14 Geometry and problem solving   **157**

14a   Classifying 2-D shapes   157
14b   3-D and 2-D shapes   159
14c   Working with coordinates   163
14d   Transformations   165

Unit 15 Problem solving and review   **168**

15a   Problem solving   168

Mathematical dictionary   **172**

I am Orlando.

Introduction

Explore the picture or problem.

What do you see? What can you find?

Key words are in a list for you to learn.

Learn new maths skills with your teacher. Look at the pictures and diagrams to help you.

Practise the maths you have learnt. Write any answers in your exercise book.

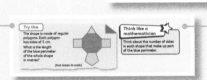

Try this challenge activity to make you think carefully about the maths.

Read these hints and tips to help you **think like a mathematician**.

At the end of each unit try the **self-check** activities. What have you learnt?

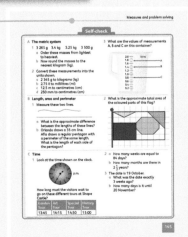

Unit 1 Number and problem solving

1a Place value and the number system

Explore

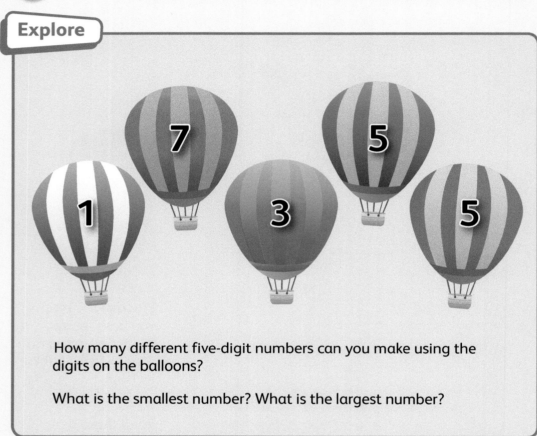

How many different five-digit numbers can you make using the digits on the balloons?

What is the smallest number? What is the largest number?

Key words

place value
digit
place holder
zero
thousand
hundred
tens
units
multiply
position
partition

Digit values

Learn

We use a place value grid to show the position and value of the digits in a number.

Hundred thousands	Ten thousands	Thousands	Hundreds	Tens	Units
	1	7	3	5	5

The digit 1 is in the ten thousands position. You know its value when you multiply 1 by 10 000.
The digit 7 is in the thousands position. You know its value when you multiply 7 by 1 000.

Practise

1 What is the value of the underlined digit in each number? Here is an example.

17 3̲36   The 7 is in the thousands position. Its value is 7 thousand.

a 40 5̲29
   45 2̲90
   405 2̲90

b 20 2̲02
   202 2̲02
   212 2̲12

c 71 3̲36
   31 7̲36
   371 3̲36

2 Write a five-digit number that has:

a six in the thousands position, for example, 26 105

b six in the thousands position and four in the hundreds position

c four in the hundreds position and nine in the tens position

d eight in the ten thousands position and four units

e 80 thousands and four units.

Try this

Write the missing digits so that the numbers in each row are in order from smallest to largest.

a 540 209   54☐200   542 145   5421☐5

b 234☐78 234 112   235 999   23☐125

c ☐99 999 601 213   6☐4 000   613 999

Partitioning numbers

Learn

We can partition a number in many different ways as long as the sum of the partitioned parts is still equal in value to the whole. You can use place value to help.

Here are a few examples.

43 512
40 000 + 3 000 + 500 + 10 + 2
43 000 + 512
40 000 + 3 500 + 12

Can you think of another way to partition 43 512?

Practise

1 Partition these numbers. The first one has been done for you.

a 43 512 =

   40 000 + 3 000 + 500 + 10 + 2

b 34 512 =

c 37 215 =

d 37 021 =

e 143 512 =

2 True or false? Write a correct answer for any answer you think is false.

a	48 017 = 40 000 + 8 000 + 100 + 7
b	248 017 = 200 000 + 40 000 + 10 + 7
c	208 107 = 200 000 + 80 000 + 107
d	308 117 = 308 000 + 117
e	23 250 = 23 000 + 250
f	23 250 = 23 000 + 200 + 50
g	23 250 = 20 000 + 3 200 + 5
h	423 502 = 40 000 + 23 000 + 500 + 2

3 Write the missing amounts.

a $56 405 = $56 000 + $☐

b $☐ = $50 000 + $6 000 + $405

c $70 388 = $70 000 + $300 + $☐

d $70 388 = $70 000 + $☐ + $8

e $156 405 = $100 000 + $☐ + $6 000 + $405

f $156 405 = $☐ + $6 000 + $405

Try this

Start with the number 638 415 each time.

Use a pencil and a paper clip to make a spinner.

Spin to find the number of parts you must use to partition 638 415.

Record the way you partition the number each time.

If you spin the same number more than once, you must partition 638 415 in a different way.

Remember to check that each partitioning is still equal in value to 638 415.

Think like a mathematician

Use a calculator to check that your parts have the same total value as your whole number.

Multiplying and dividing by 10 and 100

Learn

Hundred thousands	Ten thousands	Thousands	Hundreds	Tens	Units		Tenths	
		4	7	2	5	•		
	4	7	2	5	0	•		4725 × 10
4	7	2	5	0	0	•		4725 × 100
			4	7	2	•	5	4725 ÷ 10

Multiplying by 10 makes a quantity ten times larger.

Multiplying by 100 makes a quantity one hundred times larger.

Multiplying by 1 000 makes a quantity one thousand times larger.

What do you notice about the way the digits move each time to show how the number 4 275 has been scaled?

Remember that zero plays an important role because it keeps the other digits in the number in the correct place.

Practise

1 Solve the calculations. Work down the columns. The first one has been done for you.

a $3\,682 \times 10 = 36\,820$

$3\,682 \times 100 =$

$3\,682 \times 10 \times 10 =$

$3\,682 \times 1\,000 =$

b $4\,561 \times 10 =$

$45\,610 \div 10 =$

$45\,610 \div 100 =$

$45\,000 \div 1\,000 =$

c $36\,802 \div 10 =$

$36\,802 \div 100 =$

$36\,802 \div 10 \div 10 =$

$36\,800 \div 1\,000 =$

2 a Choose a number from the top row and an operation from the bottom row.

Make at least ten different calculations using each number and operation once at least.

| 347 | 3 470 | 6 705 | 67 050 | 67 005 |

| × 10 | × 100 | × 10 ÷ 10 | ÷ 10 | ÷ 100 |

b Give your calculations to a friend to complete.

Try this

The answer to a calculation is 3 568.

Make this answer by choosing a number and one or more of these operations. Try to find at least eight different ways to make this answer.

| × 10 | ÷ 10 | × 100 | ÷ 100 |

Now try to make calculations with the answer 12 480.

Think like a mathematician

Do not forget that zero is used as a place holder. In the number 35 680, zero holds the other digits in the correct position so that their value is known.

1b Rounding and estimating

Explore

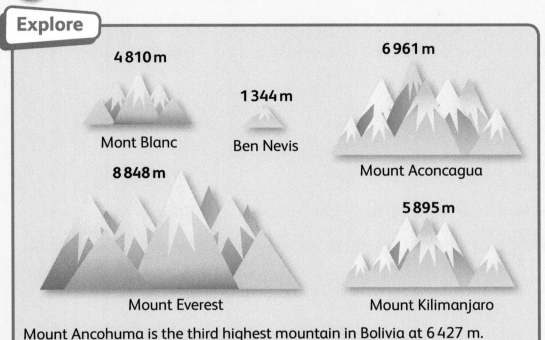

4 810 m Mont Blanc

1 344 m Ben Nevis

6 961 m Mount Aconcagua

8 848 m Mount Everest

5 895 m Mount Kilimanjaro

Mount Ancohuma is the third highest mountain in Bolivia at 6 427 m.
Is it higher or lower than each of the mountains you can see here?

Key words

place value
position
estimate
round
nearest
multiple of ten
greater than
less than

Rounding to the nearest 10

Learn

You can use rounding to make estimations. To round a number to the nearest multiple of ten, first identify the previous multiple and the next multiple of ten.

You can use this diagram for the number 1 344 to help you.

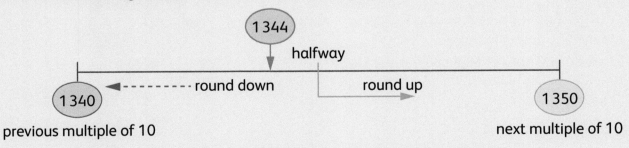

previous multiple of 10

next multiple of 10

Check to see where the number is positioned between these two multiples of ten.

A number that is less than halfway, rounds down to the previous ten.

A number that is exactly halfway or more, rounds up to the next ten. Is 1 345 less than halfway or exactly halfway to 1 350?

Practise

1 Choose a number each time to make these statements true.

When rounded to the nearest multiple of 10:

a _____ rounds up to 4 520

b _____ rounds down to 4 520

c $_____ rounds down to $2 000

d $_____ and $_____ each round to $4 500.

2 The table shows the number of litres of petrol sold at a service station during a week.

	Monday	Tuesday	Wednesday	Thursday	Friday	Saturday	Sunday
Litres sold	2 347 ℓ		2 496 ℓ	3 004 ℓ	2 865 ℓ	3 791 ℓ	2 508 ℓ

a On which day did the service station sell 2 500 ℓ rounded to the nearest ten litres?

b Round the total weekend sales to the nearest ten litres.

c Sales on Tuesday round to a multiple of 50 ℓ to the nearest ten litres.

Explain how you know that 2 855 ℓ was not sold on this day.

Try this

Round the height of each mountain in the picture on page 11 to the nearest ten metres.

Now use your rounding to estimate which of these mountains is closest in height to Mount Ancohuma in Bolivia.

What do you notice? Explain your thinking to a friend.

6 427 m

Mount Ancohuma

Comparing and ordering numbers

Learn

Hundred thousands	Ten thousands	Thousands	Hundreds	Tens	Units
2	3	4	9	1	5
2	3	4	7	9	4

Look at the two numbers here. What is the same? What is different?

The hundreds position is important as it shows us that the top number has two hundreds more than the bottom number.

You can write 234 915 > 234 794 to show that 234 915 is greater than 234 794.

You can write 234 794 < 234 915 to show that 234 794 is less than 234 915.

Practise

1 Represent each pair of numbers on a place value grid and compare them.
   Which is larger? Use the symbols < and > to show what you found out.

   a 560 123 and 560 184   b 146 235 and 142 235

   c 25 644 and 256 442   d 702 222 and 699 999

2 Put each set of numbers in order from smallest to largest.

   a 560 123   560 184   559 100   559 010

   b 146 235   149 203   142 235   149 023

   c 100 677   25 644   256 442   199 450

   d 702 222   699 929   699 999   77 975

Think like a mathematician

When you are comparing numbers, first check to see if the numbers are both whole numbers, and whether they have the same or a different number of digits.

1c Addition and subtraction

Key words

place value
addition
sum
total
subtraction
difference
estimate
inverse

Explore

Approximately how many metres does the yellow team have left to row?

Which two rowers in the yellow team have a total weight in kilograms (kg) that is a multiple of ten?

Yellow team

Rower 1: 88 kg
Rower 2: 79 kg
Rower 3: 96 kg
Rower 4: 81 kg

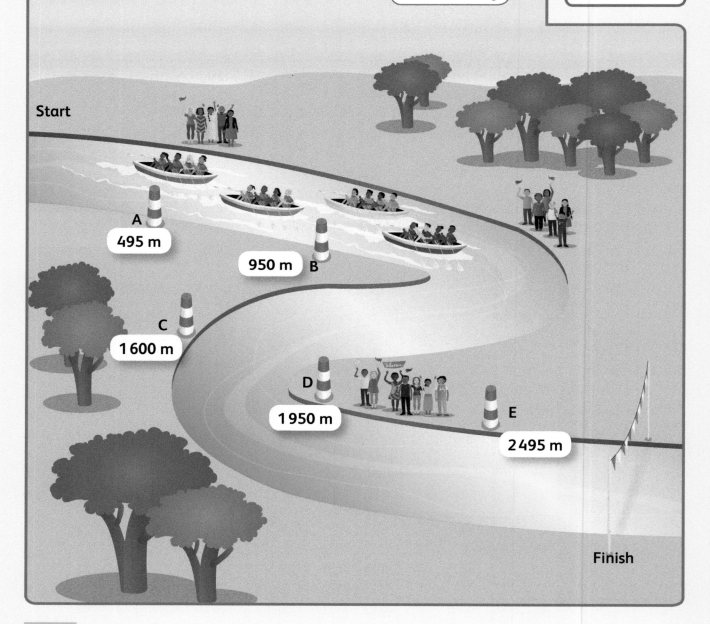

Start

A
495 m

950 m   B

C
1600 m

D
1950 m

E
2495 m

Finish

Mental addition and subtraction

Learn

Partitioning and knowledge of number bonds helps you to calculate mentally.
Here are two representations to show adding 87 and 76.

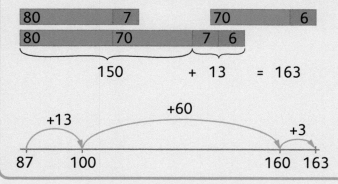

| 80 | | 7 | | | 70 | | 6 |

| 80 | | 70 | | 7 | 6 |

150   + 13   = 163

+13   +60   +3

87   100   160   163

You can use the inverse to check the answer using subtraction.
163 − 76 = 163 − 63 − 13

What do you know about the answer to 187 + 76?

Practise

1 Do the calculations using the bars and the number line representations each time.

   a 65 + 52 =   b 65 + 152 =   c 94 + 48 =   d 294 + 148 =

   Write the inverse calculations and check all your answers.

2 Pick a number from the square and a number from the circle to add together each time.
Make up and answer six additions in this way.

123	68
345	72
87	49

77	125
96	228
61	36

   Choose to use the bar or the number line representation to help you to calculate.

3 Here are the weights of some of the rowers in the boat race.
Write the missing information for each team.

	Team	Rower 1	Rower 2	Total
a	Brown	92 kg	88 kg	
b	Green	75 kg		159 kg
c	Yellow	88 kg	79 kg	
d	Blue		96 kg	177 kg

Try this

Afia thinks of a two-digit number and adds 84 to it.

Orlando thinks of a three-digit number and subtracts 84 from it.

They both write down the same three-digit number between 140 and 170 as their answer.

a What is the smallest starting number for each child?

   What is the largest starting number for each child?

b What other starting numbers can they each have?

Using a written method of addition

Learn

When there are too many steps to do a mental calculation, you can use a written calculation. Number bonds come in handy, too.

You can also add the numbers in a different order to check that your answer is correct.

For example, 132 + 58 = 190

190 + 75 = 265.

Practise

1 Complete these calculations using a written method. Look out for number bonds.

   a 45 + 63 + 72 =

   b 63 + 72 + 45 + 58 =

   c 145 + 63 + 172 =

   d 76 + 49 + 81 + 224 =

   e 276 + 89 + 41 + 24 =

2 Orlando uses rounding to help estimate the answers to the following calculations.

Will the actual answers be greater or smaller than his estimates? Why?

   a 84 + 91 + 39   estimate 80 + 90 + 40

   b 3 746 + 1 759 estimate 3 750 + 1 760

   c 5 183 + 3 254 estimate 5 180 + 3 250

3 Four customers have ordered balls of wool with these lengths.

  86 cm   95 cm   74 cm   168 cm   256 cm

Which customer has ordered the longest total length of wool?

   a    b

   c   d

   e How can you quickly work out the total length of the five different coloured balls of wool? Explain your method.

Think like a mathematician

Remember to think about any answers or information that you already know and how you can use them to help you – you do not have to recalculate each time!

Try this

Find the missing digits in these calculations.

$$\begin{array}{r} 9\ 4 \\ +\ \ 3\ \square \\ \underline{6\ 3} \\ 1\ \square\ 4 \end{array}$$

$$\begin{array}{r} 2\ 9\ 4 \\ +\ 2\ \square\ 5 \\ \underline{1\ 2\ \square} \\ 7\ 1\ 8 \end{array}$$

Choosing mental or written calculations

Learn

Start with the number 4 673.

Thousands	Hundreds	Tens	Units
4	6	7	3

Add 3 000 to 4 673. Then subtract 500 from the new answer.
Then add 50. Finally, subtract 2 486. What is the answer?
Which of these calculations could you do mentally? Why?
When did you need to use a written method?

Practise

1   Start with the number 5 374 on the place value grid each time.

Complete each set of calculations a–c and record your answers. Work down the columns.

a 5374	b 5374	c 5374
Subtract 50	Add 26	Add 400
Add 3 513	Subtract 4 000	Subtract 74
Add 2 000	Add 3 054	Subtract 300
Subtract 300	Subtract 64	Add 2 753

2   Pick a number from the triangle and a number from the circle to add together.

a   Use the numbers to make five calculations that you will solve mentally.

b   Now make up five calculations that you will solve using a written method.

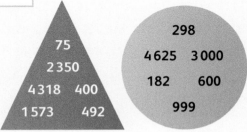

Triangle: 75, 2350, 4318, 400, 1573, 492

Circle: 298, 4625, 3000, 182, 600, 999

Think like a mathematician

When you do calculations, remember to make an estimate first and then check your answer against your estimate.

Breaking down problems

Learn

Look at this problem.

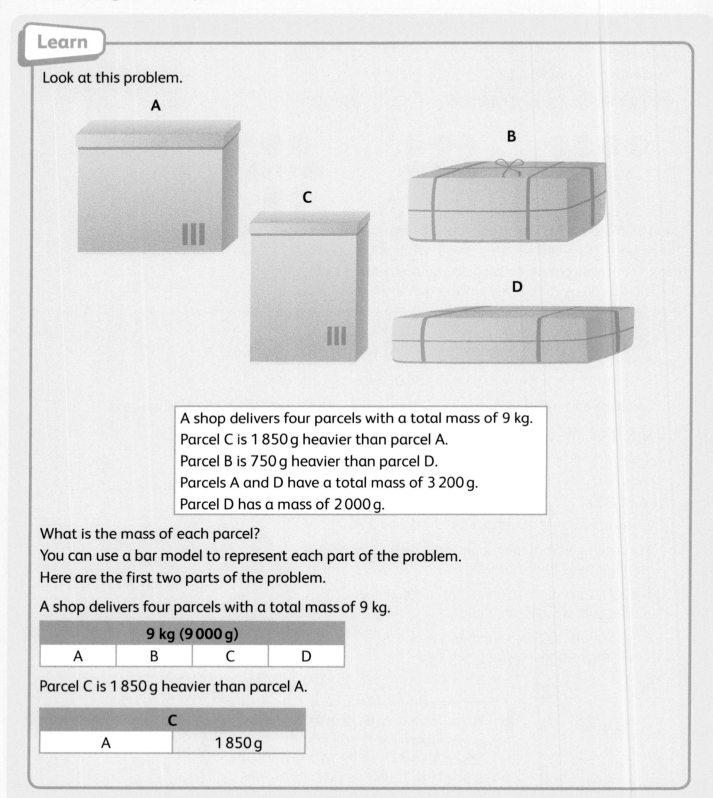

A shop delivers four parcels with a total mass of 9 kg.
Parcel C is 1 850 g heavier than parcel A.
Parcel B is 750 g heavier than parcel D.
Parcels A and D have a total mass of 3 200 g.
Parcel D has a mass of 2 000 g.

What is the mass of each parcel?

You can use a bar model to represent each part of the problem.

Here are the first two parts of the problem.

A shop delivers four parcels with a total mass of 9 kg.

9 kg (9 000 g)			
A	B	C	D

Parcel C is 1 850 g heavier than parcel A.

C	
A	1 850 g

Practise

1 Use bar models to represent the next parts of the problem:

 a Parcel B is 750 g heavier than Parcel D.

 b Parcels D and A have a total mass of 3 200 g.

 c Now use all four bar models to help you find out the mass of each parcel.

2 Solve the following problem using bar models to help you.

Afia has 3 jars of marbles.

There are 36 more red marbles than blue marbles.

The total number of blue and green marbles is 200.

Afia needs 18 more green marbles to make 100 green marbles.

How many marbles of each colour are there?

Try this

Write your own word problem to match this set of diagrams.

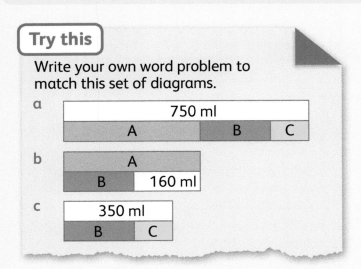

a
| 750 ml | | |
| A | B | C |

b
| A | |
| B | 160 ml |

c
| 350 ml | |
| B | C |

Self-check

A Number and problem solving

1 What is the value of the digit 3 in each of these numbers?
2<u>3</u>5 041
<u>3</u>52 041
52<u>3</u>041

2 Partition the number 235 041 in three different ways.

3 a Multiply each of these numbers by 100.
3 456
34 560
345

  b Now divide each of your answers by 10.
What do you notice?

B Rounding and estimating

1 Which of these numbers round to 4 250?
4 240   4 249   4 255   4 252   4 245

2 a Use the symbol < or > to show which number in each pair is larger.
435 344 and 453 344   443 345 and 434 543
  b Now order the four numbers from smallest to largest.

C Addition and subtraction

1 Use a mental method to complete these calculations.
a $35 + 65 + 145 =$
b $473 + 300 - 40 =$
c $6 543 - 2 000 + 57 =$

2 Use a written method to complete these calculations.
a $364 + 187 =$
b $657 + 135 + 73 =$
c $576 + 687 + 234 =$

Unit 2   Measures and problem solving

2a The metric system

Explore

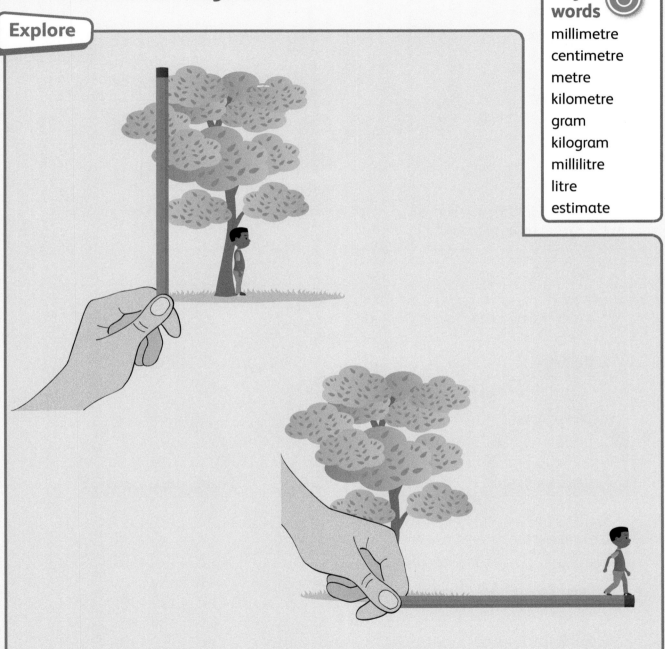

Key words ⏻

millimetre
centimetre
metre
kilometre
gram
kilogram
millilitre
litre
estimate

The world's tallest tree is a coast redwood in California, measuring more than 115 m.

How tall are the trees near your school?

Use this method to explore the heights of the trees.

Units of measurement

Learn

My height is 129 cm and I weigh 28.4 kg.

My height is one metre and thirty-one centimetres and I weigh 30.2 kg. My friend is shorter than me, but taller than Afia. His weight rounds to 29 kg.

Afia   Orlando

Explain why Orlando's friend cannot weigh 500 g less than him. Explain why Orlando's friend cannot be 20 mm taller than Afia.

Practise

1 a What is the mass on each scale?

   b Put the masses in order from lightest to heaviest.

   c Round each mass to the nearest whole kilogram.

2 a Find the values for A, B, C and D in litres and in millilitres.

   b Round each value in litres to the nearest litre.

   c Another value, E, rounds down to 3 litres when rounded to the nearest litre.
      Give a possible value for E.

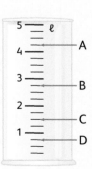

2b Length, area and perimeter

Explore

START

FINISH

How can you measure a route through this picture of a maze?

Key words
- area
- perimeter
- polygon
- regular
- formula
- centimetre squared

Length

Which line do you think is the longest? Why?

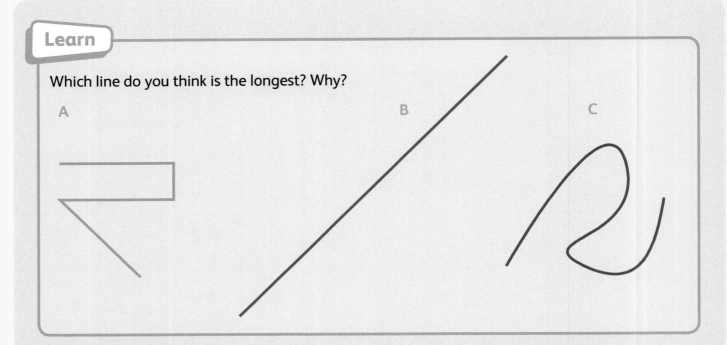

A   B   C

1 Use a ruler to draw the following lines accurately:

   a A line that is 2.5 cm longer than line B.

   b A line that is a quarter of the length of line C.

   c A line that is 2.8 cm shorter than line A.

   d A line that is 35 mm shorter than line C.

2 Complete these statements.

   a 100 cm shorter than 2.4 m is _____.

   b 45 mm longer than 30 cm is _____.

3 Afia has drawn a plan of her 'buzzer' game.

Measure the three lengths labelled on her plan.

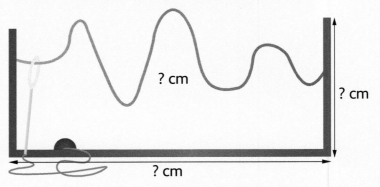

? cm

? cm

? cm

Think like a mathematician

When you work with measurements, remember always to check the units, for example 25 cm is much longer than 25 mm.

Perimeter

Perimeter is the distance or path around a two-dimensional (2-D) shape.

The perimeter of this rectangle is 12 cm.

← 3 cm →

A square is a regular shape because all four sides are equal in length and all four angles are equal in size. The perimeter of this square is also 12 cm.

What do you notice about the calculation 3 cm × 4 = and the number of equal sides of this square?

I think that we can use this information to find the perimeter of other regular polygons!

1 Find the perimeter of these squares using Afia's idea.

Check your answers using addition each time.
The first one has been done for you.

A   B   C   D

5 cm

9 cm

15 cm

25 cm

[Not drawn to scale]

Perimeter of square A = 5 cm × 4 = 20 cm

2 Write the calculation you use each time to find the perimeter of these regular shapes.

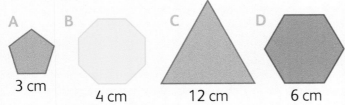

A   B   C   D

3 cm

4 cm   12 cm   6 cm

[Not drawn to scale]

What do you notice about your calculations?

Can you write a rule to help find the perimeter of any regular polygon?

3 Write the length of **one side** each time.

a The perimeter of a regular pentagon is 25 cm.

b The perimeter of a square is 20 cm.

c The perimeter of a regular octagon is 64 cm.

d The perimeter of a regular hexagon is 42 cm.

e The perimeter of a square is 18 cm.

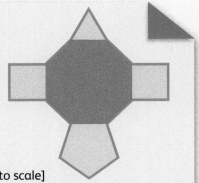

Try this

The shape is made of regular polygons. Each polygon has sides of 5 cm.

What is the length of the blue perimeter of the whole shape in metres?

[Not drawn to scale]

Think like a mathematician

Think about the number of sides in each shape that make up part of the blue perimeter.

Area

Learn

The area of a shape is the size of the surface it covers.

Area is recorded in square units, for example, square centimetres (cm^2).

You can find the area of each of these shapes by counting the squares they cover.

1 cm
1 cm

Look at the square and the rectangle. Imagine them as arrays.

What do you notice about the number of rows and columns and the total area they cover?

The square is a two-by-two array covering four squares.

The rectangle is a three-by-two array covering six squares.

You can use the formula: **area of rectangle = length × width** to help you to calculate the areas of rectangles and squares easily.

width

length

Practise

1 Find the areas of these polygons by counting the squares they cover.

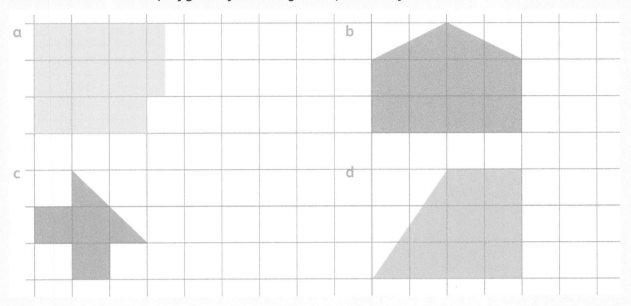

2 Find the area of each shape using the formula on page 26.

a

3 cm

4 cm

4 cm

4 cm

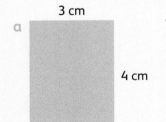

c

6 cm

2 cm

5 cm

4 cm

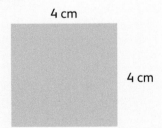

[The rectangles are not drawn to scale]

3 Orlando draws a rectangle with an area of 24 cm².

What could the length and width of the rectangle be?

Find more than one solution.

2c Time

Explore

Key words

second
minute
hour
day
week
fortnight
analogue clock
digital clock
duration
interval
calendar
timetable

You can make journeys using many different types of transport.
Estimate how long you think each journey would take – seconds, minutes, hours or days?

Using clocks and calendars

Learn

 am

Leave home

Arrive at Gran's house

How long did the journey take from my home to Gran's house?

The calendar shows the day when Orlando visited his Gran.

APRIL						
Mon	Tues	Wed	Thurs	Fri	Sat	Sun
30	31	1	2	3	4	5
6	7	8	9	10	11	12
13	14	15	16	17	18	19
20	21	22	23	24	25	26
27	28	29	30			

He will visit her again in two weeks' time. What day and date will this be?

Practise

1 Calculate the intervals between these times.

a  p.m.

b a.m.

c  p.m.

d

2 The interval between a morning time and an afternoon time is 2 hours 25 minutes.

What could the two times be? Find two different solutions.

3 Look at the calendar. What is the date?

a Five days before Wednesday 1 April.

b Five days after the last day of March.

c A fortnight before 27 April.

d 48 hours after 12 April.

Timetables

Learn

Bus and train timetables use the 24-hour clock.

Why do you think they use this clock and not the 12-hour clock?

Here are some of the stops on the green and blue bus routes.

Route	Crossley station	Bridge Creek stop	Oak Village stop	Ash Town stop	Elmside station	Pebble Beach stop
Green bus	12:55	__:__	13:25	13:46	14:25	15:09
Blue bus	13:15	13:36	13:58	14:36	15:02	15:35

To work out how long each stage of the journey takes, you must calculate the time interval between stops.

Practise

1 Calculate how long these trips on the green bus route will take.

a Crossley station to Oak Village

b Ash Town to Elmside station

c Ash Town to Pebble Beach.

2 Answer these questions.

a Is the journey from Oak Village to Pebble Beach quicker on the green bus route or on the blue bus route?

b You arrive at Elmside station at 14:28. How long must you wait for the next bus to Pebble Beach?

c The next green bus leaves Crossley station at 13:55. Write the timetable for the rest of the journey to Pebble Beach. Show the times of the stops along the way.

Think like a Mathematician

Remember that you can calculate a time interval by finding the difference between a pair of times. It is easy to count up from the earlier time to the later time.

⟳ 2d Problem solving

Key words ⟳
length
weight
capacity
problem
solution
systematic
systematically

Explore

Can you solve this puzzle?
It dates back to at least the ninth century!

25 m

Once upon a time a farmer went to the market and bought a fox, a goose and a bag of beans. On his way home, he came to the bank of a river and rented a small boat, but there was a problem! The boat was only big enough for the farmer and one of his purchases – the fox, the goose or the bag of beans! But if left alone together, the fox would eat the goose, or the goose would eat the beans.

How can the farmer get himself and all the things he bought to the other side of the river?

Solving problems using measure

Learn

What is the total mass in the boat on the first crossing?

What is the total mass in the boat on the other six crossings?

84 kg   14 kg $4\frac{1}{2}$ kg $2\frac{1}{2}$ kg

Practise

1 The distance across the river in one direction is 25 metres.

   How far does each of the following travel in the boat in total?

   a The fox

   b The goose

   c The bag of beans

   d The farmer.

2 Each crossing takes 12 minutes.

   a How long do the seven crossings take in total? Give your answer in hours and minutes.

   b The farmer rests for five minutes between each crossing.

   He started his first crossing at 14:30. What time did he finish his last crossing?

Try this

The farmer discovers that the boat has a small leak! 400 ml of water enters the boat on each crossing.

The farmer empties out 250 ml of water each time he reaches a river bank.

How much water is in the boat at the end of the last crossing?

Explain your thinking and the methods you used to calculate.

Think like a mathematician

How can you represent the problem to help you solve it?

Perhaps you could draw a diagram to keep track of the crossings and the water in the boat each time.

Self-check

A The metric system

1 Round these masses to the nearest kilogram.
  a 795 g   b 1 450g   c 2.35 kg   d 2.5 kg

2 Order these capacities from smallest to largest.
  a 1 025 ml   b 1 ℓ 200 ml   c 900 ml   d 1 201 ml   e 1 ℓ 150 ml

3 Give two lengths that are between 125 cm and 1 m 26 cm on a tape measure.

B Length, perimeter and area

1 a Draw a square with sides of 6.5 cm.
   b What calculation can you use to find the perimeter of the square?
   c What is the perimeter of a regular hexagon that also has sides of 6.5 cm?

2 What is the area of a rectangle with sides of 12 cm and 7 cm?

3 What is the area of this triangle?

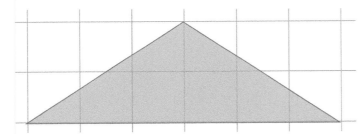

C Time

1 The pictures show two times on the same day. Which time is later?

 p.m.

2 Look at the timetable in the 'Learn' activity on page 30.
   The time is 12:55. How long must Orlando wait for the 14:25 bus?

3 The date is Friday 14 June.
   a How many weeks and days until 2 July?
   b What day of the week will 2 July be?

Unit 3   Number and problem solving

3a Number patterns

Explore

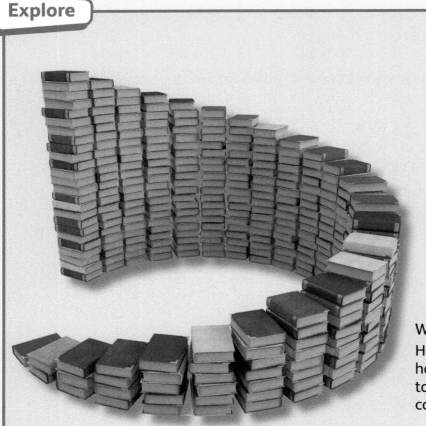

Key words
sequence
rule
term
position
next
previous
multiple
odd
even

What patterns do you notice?

How can you quickly work out how many books have been used to make the first six piles without counting all the books?

Number sequences

Learn

Number sequences follow a rule that connects each value within them.
These values are called terms.

When you count 0, 1, 2, 3, 4 …, the sequence of numbers follows the rule that the next term is always one more than the previous term. The rule is 'add one'.

In this sequence, 0 is the 1st term and 4 is the 5th term.
What is the value of the 10th term? How do you know?

Practise

1 Work out the rule for each of these sequences.
Find the 10th term each time. The first one has been done for you.

   a 0, 2, 4, 6, 8 …   0, 2, 4, 6, 8, 10, 12, 14, 16, **18**

   b 130, 125, 120, 115, 110 …

   c 0, 20, 40, 60, 80 …

   d 300, 250, 200, 150, 100 …

   e 4, $5\frac{1}{2}$, 7, $8\frac{1}{2}$, 10 …

2

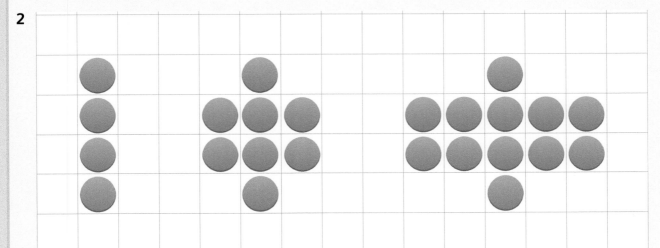

   a How many blue spots will make the next term in the sequence?

   b How do you know that one of the terms in the sequence will have 40 spots?

3 Here are three more number sequences.

Find the missing numbers. What is the rule each time?

   a 6, 12, 24, ___, ___, 192

   b 800, 400, 200, ___, 50, ___

   c $\frac{1}{4}$, $\frac{1}{2}$, ___, 2, 4, ___

Try this

Here is another sequence.

12   17   22

   a What are the values of the empty squares in this sequence?

   b What will be the value of the 4th triangle in the sequence?

   c Orlando says, '12 is in the sequence, so 120 must also be in the sequence.'

   Do you agree? Explain your thinking.

Finding multiples

Learn

Five is an odd number. It is one more than the even number four and one less than the even number six.

The picture above shows multiples of five.

Explain to a partner where you can see the multiples 5, 10, 15, and so on, in the picture.

How does the picture above show which multiples of five are odd numbers and which are even?

What does this picture show? What is the same? What is different?

Practise

1 The picture shows the first three multiples of 25.

a Write the multiples of 25 up to 250.

b Write the multiples of 50 up to 500.

c Write the multiples of 100 up to 1 000.

d What patterns do you notice? Write down some of your ideas.

2 True or false?

  a 100 is a multiple of ten, so it must also be a multiple of five.

  b 75 is a multiple of five, so it must also be a multiple of ten.

  c 40 is a multiple of five, so 400 must be a multiple of 50.

  d All multiples of ten are even numbers.

  e Multiples of five can be odd or even, so multiples of 50 can also be odd or even.

  f Multiples of 50 are also multiples of 25.

Try this

The amount of money in the car money box is a multiple of 5 cents.

The amount of money in the house money box is a multiple of 25 cents.

The amount of money in the football money box is a multiple of 10 cents.

1 Find three solutions so that:

  • the amount of money in each box is different

  • the amount of money in two boxes is the same but the amount of money in the third box is different

  • all three amounts of money are the same.

⟳ 3b **Multiplication and division**

Explore

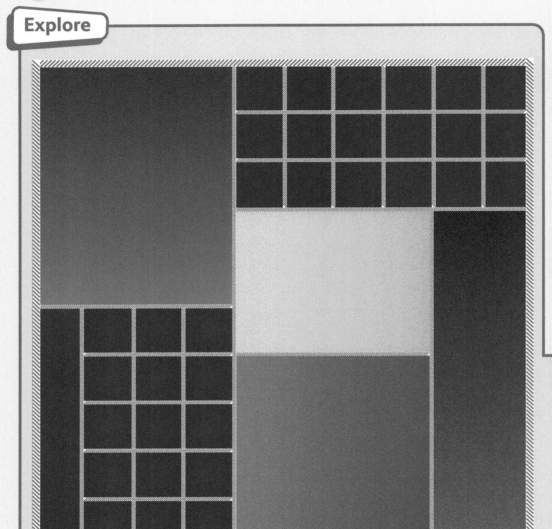

Key words ⟳
multiply
multiplication
scale
product
division
divide
divisible
quotient
remainder
square
multiple
factor

Afia makes a patchwork quilt.

How many small blue squares will be equal to the yellow patch?

How many small blue squares will be equal to the grey patch?

What other relationships can you see between the different colours on the quilt?

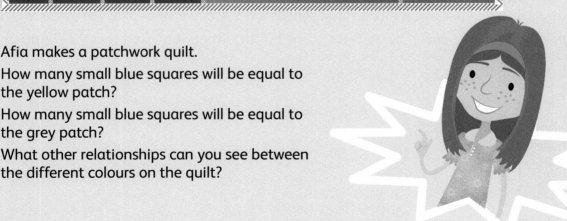

Multiplication and division facts

Learn

What facts do these images represent?

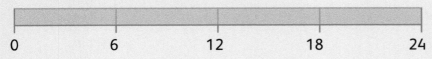

×	1	2	3	4	5	6	7	8	9	10
1	1	2	3	4	5	6	7	8	9	10
2	2	4	6	8	10	12	14	16	18	20
3	3	6	9	12	15	18	21	24	27	30
4	4	8	12	16	20	24	28	32	36	40
5	5	10	15	20	25	30	35	40	45	50
6	6	12	18	24	30	36	42	48	54	60
7	7	14	21	28	35	42	49	56	63	70
8	8	16	24	32	40	48	56	64	72	80
9	9	18	27	36	45	54	63	72	81	90
10	10	20	30	40	50	60	70	80	90	100

A multiplication square is arranged using arrays.

The grid above shows 6 × 4 = 24.

You can see how the number six has been scaled as 6 one time, 6 two times, 6 three times and 6 four times. The product of 6 four times is 24. So six four times is four times larger than 6 one time.

You can rotate the same array to represent 4 × 6 = 24

What division facts match these multiplication statements?

Practise

1 Use a multiplication grid to explore scaling.

Write the multiplication fact each time.

a 5 one time, 5 two times, 5 three times, 5 four times.

b 3 one time, 3 two times, 3 three times, 3 four times, 3 five times, 3 six times.

c 7 one time, 7 two times.

d 8 one time, 8 two times, 8 three times.

e Now write a division statement to match each multiplication fact.

2 Write two multiplication facts and two division facts to match each array.

a    **b**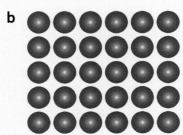

c Sketch the array that matches all four statements.

$36 \div \boxed{} = 4$

$4 \times \boxed{} = 36$

$36 \div 4 = \boxed{}$

$\boxed{} \times 4 = 36$

Remember that multiplication and division are inverse operations of each other. You can use an inverse operation to check your calculations.

3 True or false? The first one has been done for you.

a $7 + 7 + 7 + 7 = 7 \times 4$

$7 + 7 + 7 + 7 = 28$
$7 \times 4 = 28$
True.

b $7 \times 3 + 7 = 7 \times 4$

c $8 \times 5 > 5 \times 9$

d $9 + 9 + 9 + 9 + 9 = 9 \times 6$

e $30 \div 6 = 25 \div 5$

Recognising multiples

Learn

I'm thinking of a number.
It is divisible by 5.
It is also a multiple of 8.
My number is 1 less than a square number.

What number is Afia thinking of?

You can represent a square number by showing its factors, so 16 can be written as 4 × 4 or as 4^2 to show that 4 has been multiplied by itself.

So 4^2 is the same as 4 × 4, which is equal to 16.

Practise

1 (75) (300) (124) (137) (140)

Look at this set of numbers.

Find all the numbers that are:

a divisible by 10   b a multiple of 5

c divisible by 2   d divisible by 2 and 10

e not divisible by 100

f not divisible by 2, 5, 10 or 100.

2 a Complete these calculations. Work across the rows.

6 × 5 =   6 × 6 =   6 × 7 =

7 × 5 =   7 × 6 =   7 × 7 =

8 × 5 =   8 × 6 =   8 × 7 =

9 × 5 =   9 × 6 =   9 × 7 =

b Now write a number that is a multiple of six and a multiple of seven.

3 Here is a pattern of square numbers.

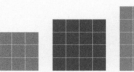

a How many small squares will you need to draw the next square number? And the next one?

b Write the missing number each time:

$10 = 3^2 + \boxed{}$ $5^2 = 35 - \boxed{}$

$7^2 + 1^2 = \boxed{}$ $10^2 = 8^2 + \boxed{}$

Think like a mathematician

It is important to first read all the information in a problem. This will help you to find the best place to start.

Try this

I'm thinking of a number.
My number is one less than a square number.
It is a multiple of seven.
It is divisible by five, but not by ten.
What number am I thinking of?

Factor pairs

Learn

I have made an array to show that 3 and 4 is the only factor pair of 12. Do you agree?

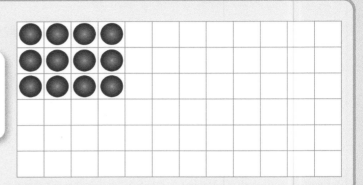

Practise

1 Look at this representation.

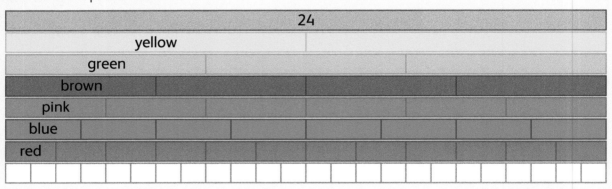

a What is the value of a yellow bar?

b What is the value of the other coloured bars?

2 Copy and complete this factor pair diagram for 24.

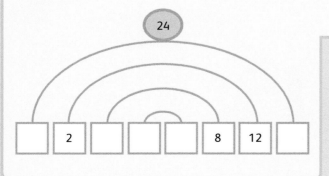

3 List all the factor pairs of:

a 15   **b** 18   **c** 30

d 42   **e** 36   **f** 17

Think like a mathematician

Use your multiplication tables to help you, but also think about factors that can and cannot be possible. For example, can an odd number have 2 as a factor?

Multiplying larger numbers

Here are two representations for the calculation 234 × 3.

Look at each part of the calculation.
What can you see that is the same?

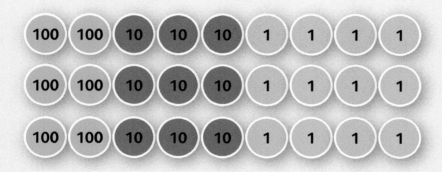

$$
\begin{array}{r}
\text{H} \quad \text{T} \quad \text{U} \\
2 \quad 3 \quad 4 \\
\times \quad \quad 3 \\
\hline
1 \quad 2 \\
9 \quad 0 \\
6 \quad 0 \quad 0 \\
\hline
7 \quad 0 \quad 2 \\
\scriptstyle 1 \quad \quad
\end{array}
$$

Now look at the calculation 34 × 13.
Where can you see each part of the calculation this time?

34 × 13 =

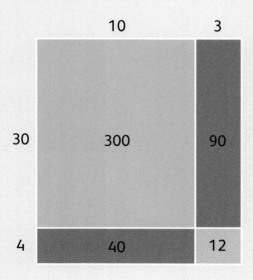

$$
\begin{array}{r}
\text{T} \quad \text{U} \\
3 \quad 4 \\
\times \quad 1 \quad 3 \\
\hline
1 \quad 2 \\
9 \quad 0 \\
4 \quad 0 \\
3 \quad 0 \quad 0 \\
\hline
4 \quad 4 \quad 2 \\
\scriptstyle 1 \quad \quad
\end{array}
$$

Practise

1 a Work out these calculations. Work down the columns.

252 × 4	345 × 4	597 × 4
252 × 6	345 × 6	597 × 6
252 × 7	345 × 7	597 × 7

   b Add the products of 234 × 4 and 345 × 4.

   Why is the answer the same as the product of 579 × 4?

   Do the other calculations work in the same way?

2 Choose a number from each shape to multiply together.

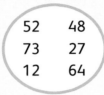

28	34
46	53
32	16

52	48
73	27
12	64

   a How many different calculations can you make with a product that is less than 1 000?

   b How many different calculations can you make with a product that is greater than 2 000?
      Use rounding to make an estimate first.

Try this

275 ml

360 ml

495 ml

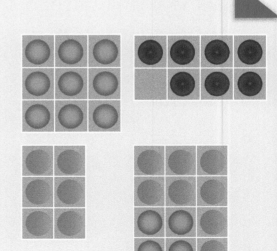

The different bottles of juice are arranged in these four crates.

Can you work out how many millilitres of juice are in each crate?

Dividing larger numbers

Learn

Here are two representations for the calculation 694 ÷ 3.

```
    2 3 1 r 1
3 | 6 9 4
```

Look at each part of the calculation.

What can you see that is the same?

There is a remainder of one because another group of three ones cannot be made.

So: 694 ÷ 3 = 231 r 1

Practise

1 Look at each calculation and decide if there will be a remainder.

   a 164 ÷ 4 =   b 484 ÷ 4 =   c 485 ÷ 4 =

   d 545 ÷ 5 =   e 546 ÷ 5 =   f 338 ÷ 3 =

   Now complete the calculations to see if you were correct.

2 What is the value of the shaded bar each time?
   Write the calculations that you use.

   a 655   b 496   c 194   d 328

   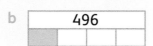

3 379 is divided into equal groups.

   a What remainders can you find?

   b Are any remainders the same? Why?

3c Problem solving

Key words

estimate
round
check
multiplication
product
division
remainder
systematic

If there are 48 rows with 65 seats in each row, can you estimate the total number of seats?

If there are 52 rows with 68 seats in each row, can you estimate the total number of seats?

Multiplication and division problems

Learn

Afia and Orlando are solving this problem:

How many days are there in 4 years?

They each use bar models to represent the problem.

Orlando's model is incorrect. How do you know?

1 year	365					
4 years	365	365	365	365	+1	Afia

1 year	365					
4 years					+1	Orlando

Why do you think that Afia and Orlando **add 1** to their answer?

Practise

1 Look carefully at the following number of days. How many whole weeks are there?

Will you use a mental or written method?

a 497 days

b 350 days

c 700 days

d 423 days

e 849 days

f 217 days

2 Use bar models to represent these calculations.

a How many days are there in 132 weeks?

b How many hours are there in 18 days?

c How many weeks are there in 553 days?

d How many hours are there in 480 minutes?

3 Here are the perimeters of some regular shapes.

What is the length of one side of each shape?

a

Perimeter
384 cm

b

Perimeter
288 cm

c

Perimeter
432 cm

[The shapes are not drawn to scale]

Think like a mathematician

Remember to make an estimate first so that you know if a solution is possible.
Do not waste time working out calculations that cannot possibly have a solution.

Try this

Use the information about the shape perimeters in question 3 to solve this problem.

How many triangles have the same perimeter as six hexagons?

How many triangles have the same perimeter as six squares?

Self-check

A Number sequences

1 The second term in a sequence is 18. The rule is **add 7**.
What are the first five terms in the sequence?

2 a What is the rule for this sequence?
350, 325, 300, 275, 250, 225
b How do you know that 120 will not be in this sequence?

B Multiplication and division

1 What are the related multiplication and division facts each time?
a 7×8
b $24 \div 3$
c 9×4
d $36 \div 6$

2 Find two different numbers each time that are:
a divisible by 5, but not divisible by 2
b divisible by 10, but not divisible by 100
c divisible by 2, but not divisible by ten.

3 Find all the factor pairs for 32.

4 Complete these calculations.
a $437 \times 6 =$
b $736 \div 3 =$
c $592 \times 8 =$
d $888 \div 6 =$

Unit 4   Geometry and problem solving

 4a Classifying 2-D shapes

Key words

scalene
isosceles
equilateral
right-angled
vertex
vertices
polygon
reflective symmetry
rotational symmetry

Explore

The wheel moves through a full turn.
How many times will the position of the spokes look the same on each wheel?

Classifying triangles

Learn

Every triangle has three sides and three vertices, or corners.

The angles in any triangle always add up to 180°, but triangles can look different.

What is the same and what is different about each of these triangles?

Equilateral

Scalene

Isosceles

Isosceles

Practise

1 Afia makes a sequence of different triangles: Isosceles, equilateral, scalene, isosceles, equilateral, scalene …

She continues this pattern using these three triangles.

a   b   c

Write the letter labels to show the order in which Afia should use them to continue the pattern.

2 The total length of the three sides of a triangle is 30 cm.

a What is the length of each side if the triangle is equilateral?

b What are some possible lengths of each side if the triangle is isosceles?

c What are some possible lengths of each side if the triangle is scalene?

Reflective and rotational symmetry

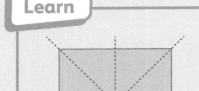

A square has **reflective symmetry**. A mirror can be placed in four positions so that one half is the reflection of the other. A square has four lines of symmetry.

A square also has **rotational symmetry** because it looks the same when you turn it about its centre point. The number of positions in which it looks exactly the same gives you its order of rotational symmetry.

Practise

1 Copy and complete the table. Use a ruler to draw the shapes.

Name of polygon					
Number of lines of symmetry	3				

2 Copy this Venn diagram. Draw the shapes in the correct place.

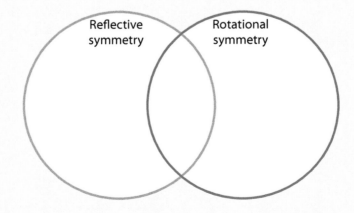

4b 3-D and 2-D shapes

Explore

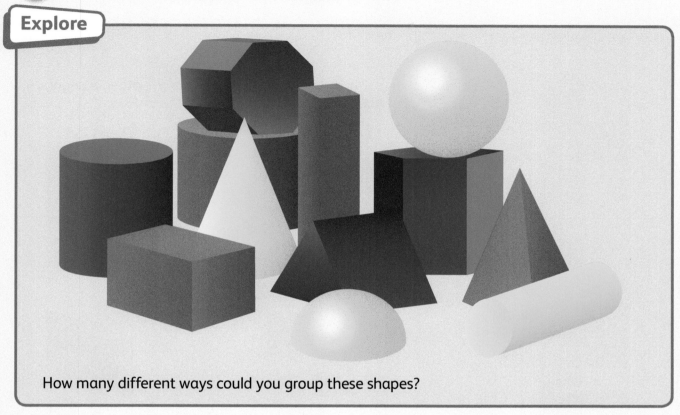

How many different ways could you group these shapes?

Nets

Learn

A net is a two-dimensional pattern of polygons that can be folded to form a three-dimensional shape.

Here are two cubes and their nets.
What is the same and what is different about them?

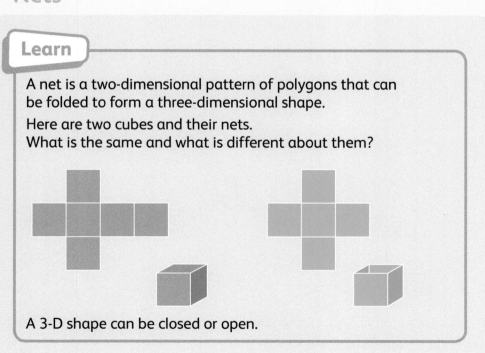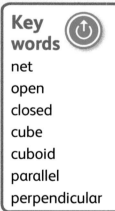

A 3-D shape can be closed or open.

Key words

net
open
closed
cube
cuboid
parallel
perpendicular

Practise

1 Which is the odd one out? Why?

a

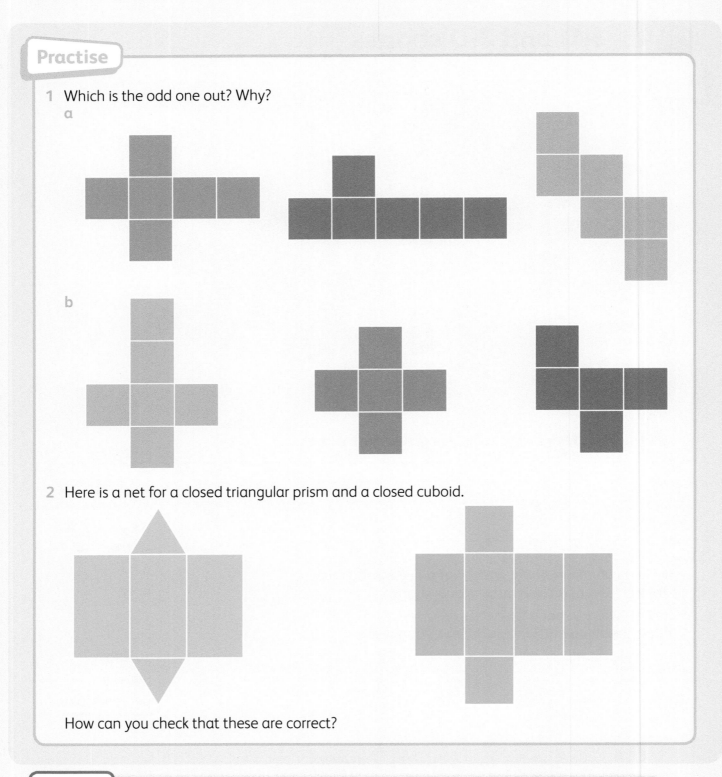

b

2 Here is a net for a closed triangular prism and a closed cuboid.

How can you check that these are correct?

Parallel and perpendicular lines

Learn

Parallel lines never meet, no matter how long they are.
A pair of **perpendicular** lines meet at a right angle (90°).
You can explore parallel and perpendicular lines in 2-D shapes.

Practise

1 Which of these shapes has:

  a perpendicular lines, but no parallel lines

  b both parallel and perpendicular lines

  c parallel lines only

  c both parallel and perpendicular lines

  d neither parallel nor perpendicular lines?

2 a What shapes can Orlando be thinking of?

  b What shapes can Orlando not be thinking of?

I am thinking of another shape with perpendicular lines.

4c Working with coordinates

Explore

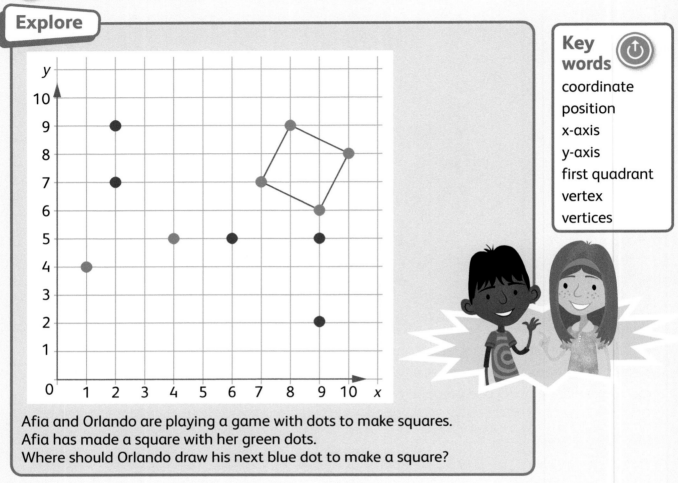

Afia and Orlando are playing a game with dots to make squares.
Afia has made a square with her green dots.
Where should Orlando draw his next blue dot to make a square?

Key words

coordinate
position
x-axis
y-axis
first quadrant
vertex
vertices

Using coordinates in the first quadrant

Learn

- Coordinates are used to show the position of a point on a flat, two-dimensional surface called a coordinate grid.

- A coordinate grid has two axes that are perpendicular to each other. These axes are the *x*-axis and the *y*-axis.

- The coordinates show a point's reference on each axis. We write the coordinates as a pair inside brackets (*x*, *y*).

- The coordinates (4, 5) describe a point that is a distance of 4 along the *x*-axis and a distance of 5 along the *y*-axis.

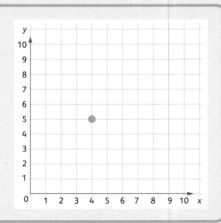

Practise

1 Find the coordinates. The first one has been done for you.

   a What are the coordinates of Afia's green dots on the coordinate grid on page 54?

   Afia's first green dot is at coordinates (1, 4).

   b What are the coordinates of Orlando's blue dots?

2 Here are some shapes on a coordinate grid.

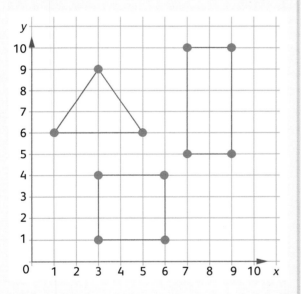

   a What are the coordinates of the vertices (corners) of each shape?

   b Give the other three coordinates for a new square with one vertex at (8, 1).

   Is there more than one possible set of coordinates for the square?

Try this

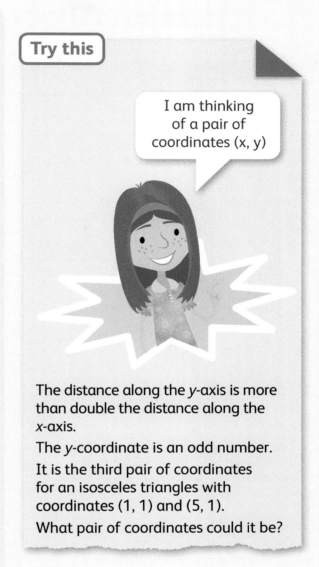

I am thinking of a pair of coordinates (x, y)

The distance along the *y*-axis is more than double the distance along the *x*-axis.

The *y*-coordinate is an odd number.

It is the third pair of coordinates for an isosceles triangles with coordinates (1, 1) and (5, 1).

What pair of coordinates could it be?

Think like a mathematician

Try to remember what you know about the properties of an isosceles triangle to help you with the problem in 'Try this'.

4d Transformations

Explore

Part of this photograph is missing because the whole person cannot be seen.

Can the reflection help you describe the missing part of the photograph? Say how.

Key words

transformation
reflection
mirror line
translation

Reflections

Learn

We describe a simple **transformation** as moving a shape so that it is in a different position, but it still has the same size, area and angles.

The basic transformations are flips (reflections), turns (rotations) and slides (translations).

Here are some reflections:

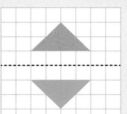 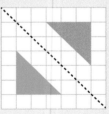

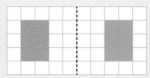

In a reflection, the shape is 'flipped'. The reflected shape is the same distance from the mirror line. Mirror lines can be horizontal, vertical or diagonal and may also be inside the shape.

Practise

1   Here are some more shapes reflected in a
    vertical mirror line.

    Are they all reflected correctly?
    How do you know?

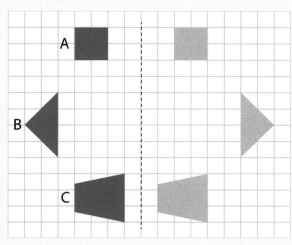

2   An irregular pentagon is reflected in a
    diagonal mirror line on a coordinate grid.

    What are the coordinates of the reflected
    shape?

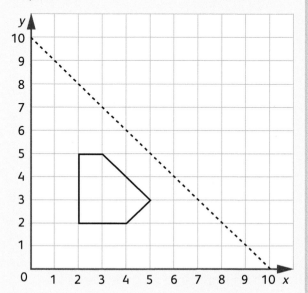

3   A quadrilateral is reflected in a horizontal
    mirror line on a coordinate grid.

    What are the coordinates of the reflected
    shape?

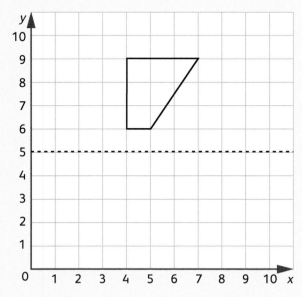

Translations

Learn

A **translation** is a movement along a straight line. A shape can be translated up or down, left or right, or in a combination of a number of moves.

The shape does not rotate or change its size or the way it looks. In fact it looks exactly the same.

In this diagram, the rectangle is shown in its original position.

The translation of this rectangle to position A is described as **3 squares right and 4 squares up**. All four vertices of the rectangle translate in this way.

The translation of the original rectangle to position B is described as **6 squares right** as there is no move in a vertical direction.

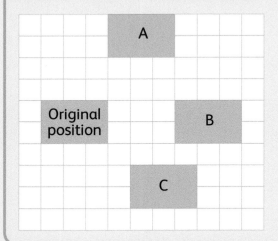

Practise

1 Describe the following translations:
   a original position to position C
   b position B to the original position
   c position A to the original position
   d position A to position B
   e position B to position C.

2 A triangle is translated on a grid.
   a Which shape shows the triangle after the translation?
   b Describe the translation.

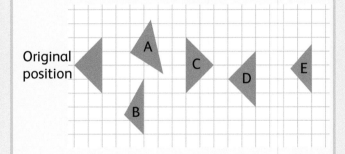

Try this

You will need some squared paper.

1 Draw a rhombus and label it O for original position.

   Translate it 1 square right and 2 squares down. Label it A.

   Translate shape A by moving it 2 squares right and 3 squares down. Label it B.

   Translate shape B by moving it 3 squares right and 4 squares down. Label it C.

   a Can you predict the position of translated shape D? And E?

      What patterns do you notice?

   b Describe the translation to return shape E to the original position O.

For the 'Try this' activity, think about the way that the number of squares used for each translation changes each time.

⟳ 4e **Problem solving**

Explore

Which different shapes and lines can you see on this old railway bridge?

Solving problems

Key words ⟳

properties of shapes
solution
nets
parallel lines
perpendicular lines
reflective symmetry
rotational symmetry

Learn

Vans, trains, boats and aeroplanes can transport letters, parcels and other cargo around the world.

Here are some of the boxes ready to be shipped.

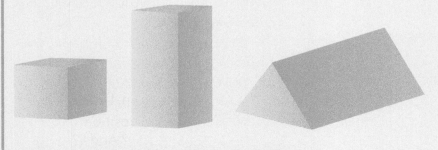

What could the nets of each box look like?

Practise

1 Carefully draw a net for each of the boxes on page 59.

2 A new delivery company 'Parcels on the Move' is designing its **logo** using **three** different 2-D shapes. The design must include:

- one shape with reflective symmetry and rotational symmetry
- at least one shape with no rotational symmetry
- two shapes with parallel lines
- at least one shape with a pair, or pairs, of perpendicular lines
- a scalene triangle.

Sketch a logo design for the new company.

3 The company is planning the day's delivery route. The coordinate grid shows the places where parcels must be delivered.

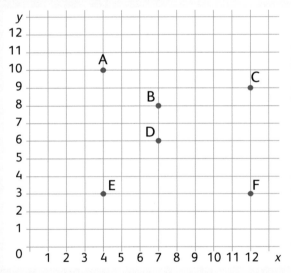

a What are the coordinates for each place?

b The last delivery place (G) is at location (1, 5).

Two drivers will deliver the seven parcels between them.

One driver follows a route that makes an **isosceles triangle**.

The other driver follows a route that makes a **rectangle**.

Which locations did each driver visit?

Think like a mathematician

Remember to use what you know about properties of shapes to help you.

Try this

The two drivers follow the same-shaped routes on the following day.

However, each vertex (corner) on the rectangular route is translated four squares right and one square up.

The triangular route is reflected in a vertical mirror line that cuts through the x-axis at (6, 0).

1 What are the new coordinates for each route?

2 The driver of the rectangular route gives a parcel to the other driver. Why?

How should this driver's route be changed now that he has fewer parcels to deliver? What shape will this changed route make?

Self-check

A Classifying 2-D shapes

1 What is the name of each of these triangles?

a
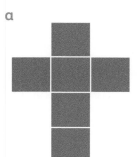
b

c

2 Which of these polygons have both reflective and rotational symmetry?
a Regular hexagon
b Equilateral triangle
c Rectangle
d Isoceles triangle.

B 3-D and 2-D shapes

1 Afia wants to send a parcel. Which net can she use to make a closed cube-shaped box?

a   b   c

2 Name a different 2-D shape each time that has:
a one or more pairs of parallel lines
b at least one pair of perpendicular lines
c both parallel and perpendicular lines
d no parallel lines and no perpendicular lines.

C Working with coordinates

1 a Plot the following points on a coordinate grid to make the first three vertices (corners) of a rectangle: (3, 4), (7, 4) and (7, 6).

   b What is the coordinate of the fourth vertex (corner) that is needed to complete the rectangle?

D Transformations

1 Reflections

Sketch on paper, or describe the position of the triangle, to show its reflection in the mirror line.

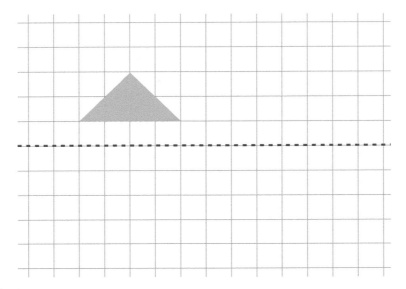

2 Translations

a Sketch on paper, or describe the position of the same triangle in the question above, after the translation 5 squares right and 5 squares down.

b Now reflect and sketch the translated triangle in the mirror line.

Unit 5   Problem solving and review

5a Problem solving

Explore

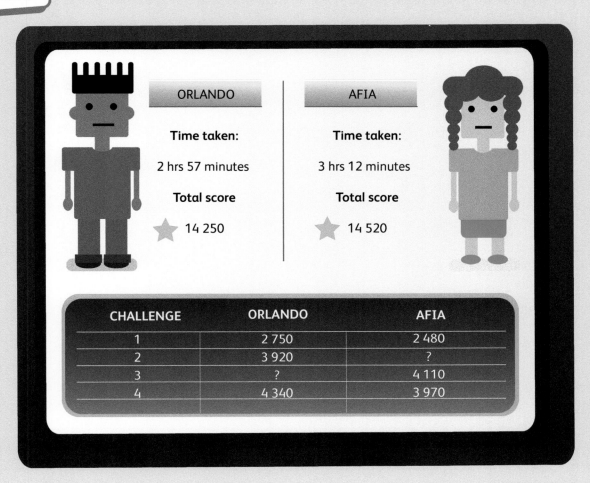

	ORLANDO	AFIA
Time taken:	2 hrs 57 minutes	3 hrs 12 minutes
Total score	⭐ 14 250	⭐ 14 520

CHALLENGE	ORLANDO	AFIA
1	2 750	2 480
2	3 920	?
3	?	4 110
4	4 340	3 970

All the problems in this unit are about our computer game.

Look at all the information here. Can you think of any word problems about the computer game?

Challenge 1

Players score points for finding paths through the 'Power-maze' by moving from one hexagon to another that is connected to it. Each path follows a pattern.

Score 500 points for a path with multiples of 25.

Score 400 points for a path with numbers **not** divisible by 5.

Score 350 points for a path with multiples of 6.

Score 250 points for a path following the rule 'subtract 7'.

1 How many points can you score in total? Write down the numbers in the paths you score on.

2 Six of the numbers on the 'Power-maze' are square numbers. Which numbers are they?

3 Can you make up your own 'Power-maze' path that follows a pattern for a friend to find?

Copy this path and remember to include some numbers that do not fit the pattern.

START

49				11	
	32		18		3
39		25		9	
	50		150		400
100		47		175	
	60		80		255
54		42		45	
	151		36		48
45		64		24	

FINISH

START

FINISH

Challenge 2

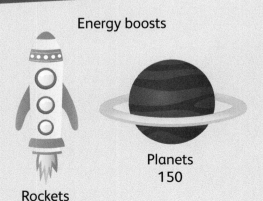

Energy boosts

Rockets
200

Planets
150

Players earn Energy boosts as they work through each challenge.

Orlando earns 2000 Energy boosts and Afia earns 1700 Energy boosts.

1 How many Rocket and Planet boosts could they each have won?

2 Afia could not have won Rocket boosts only.

Find a way to prove if this statement is true or false.

Challenge 3

The Energy boosts are shown on a grid.

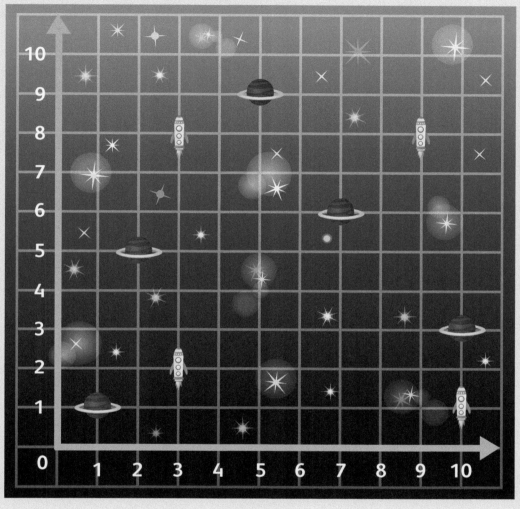

1 What are the coordinates of each of the Planet boosts?

2 There should be five of each type of boost on the grid, but one of the Rocket boosts is missing.

Its position makes a square with three of the other Rockets.

What are the coordinates of the missing Rocket boost?

3 The distance from 0 to 10 on each axis is 40 cm.

What is the perimeter of the square made by the Rocket boosts in question 2?

4 Three Planet boosts at coordinates (1, 1), (2, 5) and (7, 6) make the vertices of a triangle.

The triangle is translated 2 squares right and 3 squares up.

What are the new coordinates of the three Planet boosts now?

Challenge 4

The Spaceship Super Challenger has pods arranged in lines of three to keep the space ship balanced.

Arrange these masses in the pods on the spaceship so that the total mass of any three pods that are joined is the same.

| 320 kg | 750 kg | 380 kg | 450 kg | 810 kg | 390 kg |

Unit 6   Number and problem solving

6a Place value and the number system

Can you write all whole numbers in this way?

Partitioning numbers

Learn

3 250 − 1 759 = ?

Why do you think Orlando will partition the number in this way?

I am going to partition 1 759 into 1 000, 750 and 9 to help me.

Key words

place value
partition
digit
place holder
tenths
hundredths
decimal
whole number
multiply

Practise

1 Use all the boxes each time to partition the number.

  a 3 475 = 3 400 + ☐ + ☐

  b 63 475 = ☐ + 3 000 + ☐ + 175

  c 463 405 = 45 000 + ☐ + 400 + ☐

2 Partition these numbers into four parts each time. The first one has been done for you.

  a 12 568   It can be partitioned into 12 000, 500, 60 and 8.

  b 12 5680

  c 120 685

  d 825 005

  e 125

3 How will you partition 654 each time to complete these calculations easily?

  a 4 350 + 654 =

  b 3 554 − 654 =

  c 2 846 + 654 =

  d 9 504 − 654 =

Think like a mathematician

Remember to think about number bonds and
other facts to help you with question 2.

Try this

Afia pours 1 850 ml of juice into different jugs.
She pours a multiple of 150 ml of juice into a jug.
She pours a multiple of 100 ml of juice into a second jug.
She pours a multiple of 25 ml of juice into a third jug.
She pours 75 ml of juice into a fourth jug.

How much did she pour into each jug?
Work out at least three different solutions.

Decimal place value

Learn

A place value grid shows you the position and value of the digits in a number.

Hundreds	Tens	Units	Tenths	Hundredths
	4	8	2	5

The digit 2 is in the tenths position. You know its value when you divide two units by ten.

The digit 5 is in the hundredths position. You know its value when you divide five units by one hundred.

The diagram below shows the fraction of a whole that two tenths and five hundredths represent. We write this as 0.25.

How many hundredths are equal to one tenth?

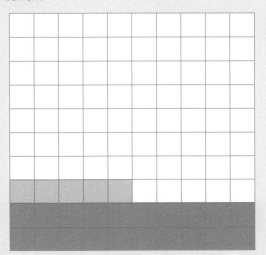

Practise

1 Show the value of each digit using partitioning. The first one has been done for you.

   a 4.5 = 4 + 0.5   b 0.45 =   c 4.45 =

   d 44.5 =   e 4.08 =   f 14.8 =

2 Complete the calculations. Work down each column.

   a 3 ÷ 10 =   b 0.2 ÷ 10 =   c 23 ÷ 10 =

      3 ÷ 100 =   0.02 × 10 =   23 ÷ 10 ÷ 10 =

      3 ÷ 10 ÷ 10 =   2 ÷ 100 =   23 ÷ 100 =

      30 ÷ 100 =   0.02 × 100 =   230 ÷ 100 ÷ 10 =

      30 ÷ ☐ = 0.3   20 ÷ 1000 =   230 ÷ ☐ = 0.23

6b Rounding and ordering

Explore

Key words

place value
estimate
round
nearest whole number
tenths
hundredths
decimal
greater than
less than
negative
positive
difference
Celsius
temperature

What questions could we ask about these pictures that start with 'How much warmer ...'?

Rounding decimal numbers

Learn

You can use rounding to make estimations.

Look at the calculations 4.8 + 4.1 and 4.82 + 4.15

a What would be good estimates for these calculations?

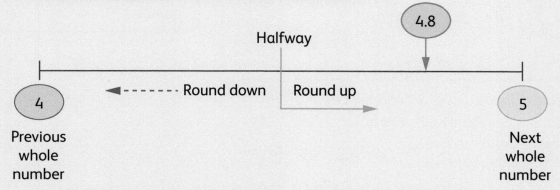

To round a number to the nearest whole number, you must first identify the previous whole number and the next whole number.

You can use the diagram for the number 4.8 to help you to decide if you should round up or round down.

b Use the diagram to explain how you know that 4.1 will round down to 4.

c Which whole numbers do 4.82 and 4.15 each round to?

Practise

1 Round to the nearest whole number. Work down the columns.

a	b	c
6.4	25.5	130.4
6.45	2.55	13.4
64.5	0.55	13.44
0.64	5.45	13.54

2 Which measurement is the odd one out each time?

a 6.45 km, 5.98 km, 6.5 km, 5.5 km round to 6 km.

b 0.75 kg, $\frac{1}{2}$ kg, 1.2 kg, 1.39 kg, 0.48 kg round to 1 kg.

c 4.2 m, 3.94 m, 3.49 m, 4.09 m round to 4 m.

d 12.43 ℓ, 12.53 ℓ, 13.2 ℓ, 13.43 ℓ, 12.9 ℓ round to ☐ ℓ.

Try this

I'm thinking of a decimal number. It rounds to 7.
I add two tenths to my number. It now rounds to 8.

Think like a mathematician

What do you know about rounding to the nearest 10 or to the nearest 100?
How can this help you to round decimals to the nearest whole number?

What could Orlando's decimal number be?

What decimal number could it not be?

Can you work out a rule?

Comparing and ordering decimal numbers

Learn

Which is larger, 1.4 or 1.24?

You can represent the decimal numbers to help you.

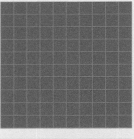
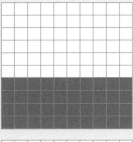

Units	Tenths	Hundredths
1	4	0

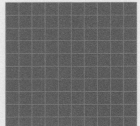
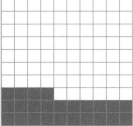

Units	Tenths	Hundredths
1	2	4

Although both numbers have 1 as the units value, 1.4 has four tenths whereas 1.24 only has two tenths. This is written as: 1.4 > 1.24 or 1.24 < 1.4

Practise

1 Compare these decimal numbers. Use < , > or = to record your answers.
   The first one has been done for you.

   a 2.3 and 3.2   2.3 < 3.2   b 2.3 and 2.32

   c 2.3 and 2.23   d 2.3 and 2.30

   e 5.45 and 5.5   f 5.4 and 4.98

   g 5.0 and 5.01

2 Order each set of values from smallest to largest.

   a 2.4 m   2.24 m   1.42 m

   b $1.75 $1.57 $1.70 $1.80

   c 10.75 kg   10.57 kg   10.7 kg   10.8 kg   10.08 kg

   d 1.1 m   1.01 m   0.11 m   0.1 m   1.11 m

Negative numbers

Learn

Positive numbers are greater than zero, and negative numbers are less than zero.
A pair of numbers such as 3 and −3 are both the **same distance** from zero.

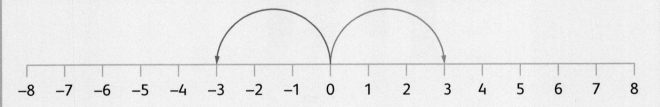

3 is greater than −3 so you can
write 3 > −3.

The difference between 3 and −3 is 6,
so the difference between the
temperatures 3°C and −3°C is 6°.

When a calculation crosses zero, it is
useful to stop at zero before counting
on or counting back.

Think like a mathematician

You can use your number bonds to help
cross zero.
Think about the different ways that
single digit numbers can be partitioned.

Practise

1 Use the number line on page 73 to decide which statements are true and which are false. Work down the columns.

a   −5 > 4

−5 < −6

−5 < 0

5 < −1

b   8 > 4 > −2

−2 < 4 < 8

−2 < −4 < −8

−2 < 0 < 2

2 Complete the following sentences to make them true:

a   5°C warmer than −1°C is _____.

b   5°C colder than −1°C is _____.

c   The difference between −6°C and 2°C is _____.

d   The difference between −3°C and _____ is 5°.

3 The chart shows the minimum and maximum temperatures for one day recorded at five different locations.

a Calculate the difference in the maximum and minimum temperatures at each location.

b The minimum temperature at Location E was 9° lower than the maximum temperature that day. Calculate the minimum temperature.

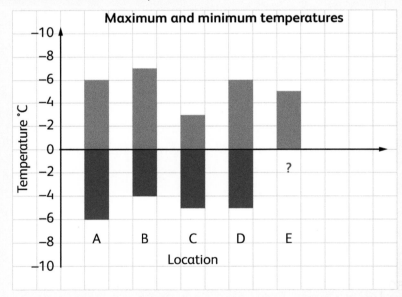

Try this

Arrange all six numbers in the diagram so that:
● numbers joined by horizontal red lines have a difference of 8
● numbers joined by vertical blue lines have a difference of 5.

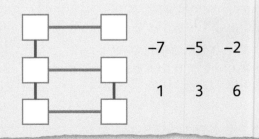

−7   −5   −2

1   3   6

6c Addition and subtraction

Key words

place value
decimal place
tenths
hundredths
addition
sum
total
subtraction
difference
estimate
inverse

Explore

I am going to spend my whole dollar!

I have $2, but I don't want to spend it all.

Choose some items that Afia and Orlando could buy. Give them each three options. Which items should not be in this shop? Add the prices of those items together.

UNDER A DOLLAR SHOP

OPEN
9:00 am
CLOSE
5:30 pm

$6.99   15c   40c   49c   90c $4.75 $0.50   80c   10c   50c   15c   30c   25c   60c $3.90 $2.49   10c   70c

Decimal pairs

Learn

The yellow rectangle represents one whole, or 1.

The second rectangle shows the whole divided into ten equal parts. Each part is worth $\frac{1}{10}$ or 0.1.

The second rectangle is also made up of two coloured parts. The blue part is made up of seven of the ten equal parts or 0.7. The yellow part is three of the ten equal parts or 0.3.

You can say 0.7 + 0.3 = 1 because seven of the equal parts add three of the equal parts is ten of these equal parts.

What else can you say?

0.1	0.1	0.1	0.1	0.1
0.1	0.1	0.1	0.1	0.1

Practise

1 Work out the addition and subtraction statements to match these images. Each whole shape is divided into ten equal parts.

a

0.1	0.1	0.1	0.1	0.1
0.1	0.1	0.1	0.1	0.1

b

0.1	0.1	0.1	0.1	0.1
0.1	0.1	0.1	0.1	0.1

c
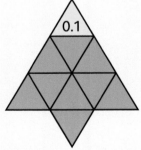

d
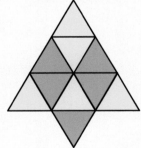

2 This number line shows 6.5 + 3.5 = 10

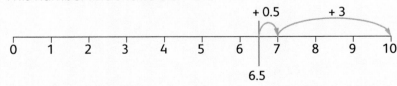

Use a number line to check each calculation. Correct any calculations that are wrong.

a 4.5 + 5.5 = 10   b 10 = 6.4 + 4.6   c 10 − 3.5 = 7.5

d 0.9 + 9.1 = 10   e 10 − 2.9 = 7.1   f 5.9 + 5.1 = 10

Try this

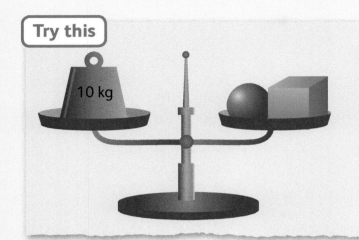

The mass of each shape is recorded to one decimal place, for example 4.3 kg.

The cube is heavier than the sphere.

The difference between their masses is less than 4 kg.

1 Write at least five ways to make this true.

2 What is the greatest mass that the cube can be?

Think like a mathematician

Check that your decimal pairs to ten are possible, by thinking about bonds to 100. For example, if you know that 65 + 35 = 100, then 6.5 + 3.5 = 10 because all values are 10 times smaller.

Using rounding to add and subtract near multiples of 10 or 100

Learn

I want to put nine more crayons in the box. I will put in a bundle of ten. What must I do next?

I want to take nine crayons from the box. I will take out a bundle of ten. What must I do next?

Afia and Orlando are both using a rounding and adjusting method to add or subtract near multiples of ten.

77

Practise

1 Complete the calculations by first adding or subtracting a multiple of 10 or 100.
  Think about what you will need to do next each time. Work down the columns.
  The first one has been done for you.

a
32 + 9 =   You know that 32 + 10 = 42,
32 + 19 =   so 32 + 9 will be one less.
132 + 19 =
132 + 49 =
132 + 99 =

b
85 − 9 =
85 − 19 =
185 − 19 =
185 − 49 =
185 − 99 =

c
64 + 8 =
64 − 8 =
64 + 18 =
64 − 18 =
164 + 98 =

2 The cost of a room in a hotel for a week is $275 dollars.
  What is the total cost for the flight and the hotel with each holiday company?

Holiday company	Sunny Dreams	Fly Away	Happy Holidays	Travel Time
Flight cost	$399	$299	$249	$295

Finding the difference between two near multiples of 10 or 100

Learn

You can use a counting up method to find the difference between two near multiples
of 10 or 100.

1 004 − 285 = 719

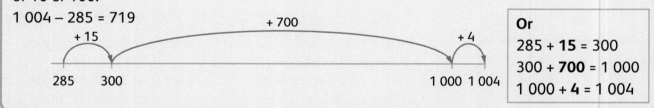

Or
285 + **15** = 300
300 + **700** = 1 000
1 000 + **4** = 1 004

Practise

1 Work out the difference between these pairs of numbers.
  Think about what you will need to do next each time.

  a 378 and 509   b 495 and 810   c 692 and 1105   d 94 and 812   e 509 and 378

2 Rounding and adjusting, or counting up? Choose which method you will use to answer
  these subtraction calculations. Be prepared to explain your decision.

  a 375 − 199 =   b 405 − 295 =   c 1210 − 990 =   d 950 − 349 =
  e 1 000 − 478 =   f 53 − 49 =   g 304 − 299 =   h 2 005 − 1 987

Adding and subtracting decimal numbers mentally

Learn

You can use mental methods or written methods to calculate with decimals.

Just like with whole numbers, you must look at the decimals carefully to help you make a decision. You should always think about number bonds and make estimates too.

6.4 + 3.7 can be solved as 6.4 + 3.6 + 0.1 using a mental method.

It can also be solved as 9 + 1.1 or 10 + 0.1 using number bonds.

68.25 + 15.75 can be solved as 68 + 15 + 1 using a mental method.

68.25 – 15.75 can be solved as 68.25 – 0.25 – 15 – 0.5 using a mental method.

68.25 – 59.95 can be solved by counting up 0.05 to 60 and then adding 8.25 to reach 68.25.

Practise

1 Use a mental method to complete these calculations.
  Use rounding to the nearest whole number to make an estimate first.
  The first one has been done for you.

  a 26.3 + 12.7 = _____ (estimate 26 + 13 = 39)   b 26.4 + 12.6 = _____

  c 26.4 – 12.4 = _____   d 26.4 + 12.8 = _____

  e 26.4 – 22.8 = _____   f 52.65 + 12.35 = _____

  g 52.65 + 12.38 = _____   h 52.65 – 48.99 = _____

2 a Make all the lengths 1.45 m longer.

    2.55 m   3.75 m   4.99 m   2.26 m

  b Make all the masses 2.8 kg lighter.

    5.8 kg   10 kg   8.4 kg   12.5 kg

Think like a mathematician

Remember to look at all the numbers first and then decide on the order you will add them.

Try this

1 Orlando and Afia are comparing the litres of rainwater they collected over three weeks.

	Week 1	Week 2	Week 3	Total
Orlando	6.35 litres	8.75 litres	3.65 litres	X
Afia	5.8 litres	Y	6.9 litres	20 litres

  a What are the values of X and Y?

  b Use the information to make up some addition and subtraction statements about the water collected. For example, Orlando collected 2.4 litres more in Week 2 than in Week 1.

Partitioning numbers

When there are too many steps to solve a calculation mentally, you can use a written method. It is important to line up the numbers carefully in the columns so the place value is correct.

It is also useful to make an estimate first.
To calculate 529.3 + 243.8, a useful estimate is 530 + 240 = 770.

```
H  T  U . 1/10
5  2  9 . 3
+ 2  4  3 . 8
7  7  3 . 1
   1     1
```

0.3 + 0.8 = 1.1

| 0.1 | 0.1 | 0.1 | 0.1 | 0.1 | | 0.1 | 0.1 | 0.1 | 0.1 | 0.1 |
| 0.1 | 0.1 | 0.1 | 0.1 | 0.1 | | 0.1 | 0.1 | 0.1 | 0.1 | 0.1 |

```
    H   T   U . 1/10
   ⁴5̶ ¹2 ⁸9 . ⑶
 − 2   4   3 . 8
   2   8   5 . 5
```

13 tenths − 8 tenths = 5 tenths
1.3 − 0.8 = 0.5

Practise

1 Use a written method to calculate these answers.
   Make an estimate first each time.

   a 345.7 + 123.6 =

   b 345.7 − 123.6 =

   c 654.3 + 262.7 =

   d 654.3 − 262.7 =

   e Choose one of the questions and use an
      inverse calculation to check your answer.

Think like a mathematician

For question 2, remember to estimate the size of the answer before calculating. If your estimate for a total is much more than $500, then you know not to waste time calculating.

2   $164.75 $349.50 $185.49 $86.73

   a Add these amounts to make at least five totals that are less than $500.

   b Subtract these amounts to calculate differences that are less than $150.

Reasoning about addition and subtraction

Learn

Afia writes down the four-digit number 7 352.

She then writes it in the reverse order 2 537.

She then calculates the sum of the two numbers 9 889.

9 889 is a **palindromic** number because it remains the same when its digits are reversed.

My number starts and finishes with the same digit, and both middle digits are the same.

Practise

1 Use these starting numbers to find more palindromic numbers.
The first one has been done for you.

   a 1 234   Write 1 234 in reverse order to get 4 321.

   1 234 + 4 321 = 5 555 which is a palindromic number.

   b 2 345   c 3 634   d 7 252

   e 3 814   f 5 241

2 Decimal numbers can also be palindromic.

   Use these starting numbers to find decimal palindromic numbers.

   a 43.21   b 54.32   c 43.63   d 3.6   e 34.25

Try this

Always, sometimes or never true?

The last answer you reach will be 6 174.

Write down a four-digit number, making sure that all the digits are not the same.
Arrange the four digits to make the largest and the smallest possible numbers.
Subtract the smallest number from the largest number.

Take the answer and rearrange the digits again to make the largest and smallest numbers.
Subtract the smallest number from the largest number.
Continue in the same way. What do you notice?

Self-check

A Place value and the number system

1 Use the information in the table to find the total number of points scored by three teams in a target game. Use a written method to help you calculate.

		Round 1	Round 2	Round 3	Round 4	Round 5	TOTAL
a	Red team	65	87	123	145	75	
b	Blue team	87	75	203	89	120	
c	Green team	220	98	85	79	103	

2 a What is the value of the digit 6 in each of these decimal numbers?
   2.6   24.6   2.46   6.24   2.64
 b Partition the number 2.46 in three different ways.
 c A number is multiplied by 1 000. The answer is 36 500. What is the number?

3 a Order this set of decimal numbers from smallest to largest.
   5.6   6.5   5.55   6.05   4.92
 b Now round each of the decimal numbers to the nearest whole number.

4 Use the symbols < and > to compare these numbers.
   a −4 and 4   b 3 and −2   c −5 and −3   d −6 and 0
 Calculate the difference between these temperatures.
   a −4°C and 4 C   b 3°C and −2°C   c −5°C and −3°C   d −6°C and 0°C

5 a What must you add to each number to total 1?
   0.7   0.3   0.5   0.1
 b What must you add to each number to total 10?
   7.7   2.3   4.5   6.1

B Rounding and ordering

1 Use rounding and adjusting to complete these calculations.
   a 125 + 49 =   b 125 − 49 =   c 345 + 198 =   d 786 − 299 =

C Addition and subtraction

1 Complete these calculations.
   a 137.8 + 23.4 =   b 137.8 − 23.4 =   c 45.72 + 16.28 =   d 45.72 − 16.28 =

Unit 7 Measures and problem solving

7a The metric system

Explore

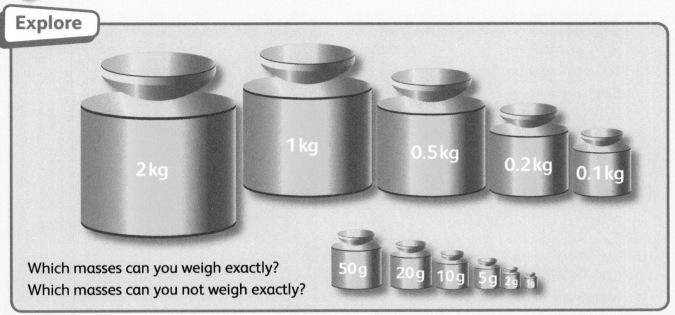

Which masses can you weigh exactly?
Which masses can you not weigh exactly?

Converting units

Learn

Term	'Centi' (hundredth)	'Milli' (thousandth)	'Kilo' (thousand)
Length	a centimetre (cm) is $\frac{1}{100}$ of a metre (m)	a millimetre (mm) is $\frac{1}{1\,000}$ of a metre (m)	a kilometre (km) is a thousand metres

What do you know about a kilogram?

What do you know about a millilitre?

You can multiply or divide values by 10, 100 or 1 000 to help you convert between units of measurement. The relationship between the sizes of the units is what tells you this.

For example, a gram (g) is $\frac{1}{1\,000}$ of a kg, or you can say that there are 1 000 grams in a kilogram.

$3\,500\,g \div 1\,000 = 3.5\,kg$ and $2.4\,kg \times 1\,000 = 2\,400\,g$

Key words

millimetre
centimetre
metre
kilometre
gram
kilogram
millilitre
litre
estimate

Practise

1 Convert these measurements.

Mass	Length	Capacity
4 kg to grams (g)	10 cm to millimetres (mm)	2 ℓ to millilitres (ml)
3 000 g to kilograms (kg)	45 cm to metres (m)	1 600 ml to litres (ℓ)
1.5 kg to grams (g)	4.5 m to centimetres (cm)	1.5 ℓ to millilitres (ml)
1 600 g to kilograms (kg)	450 m to kilometres (km)	275 ml to litres (ℓ)
0.75 kg to grams (g)	4.5 km to metres (m)	0.25 ℓ to millilitres (ml)

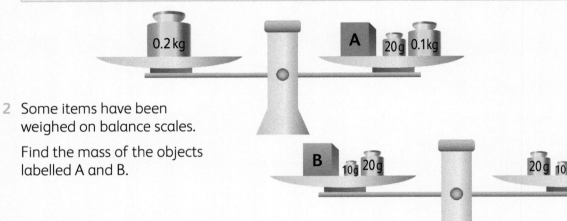

2 Some items have been weighed on balance scales.

Find the mass of the objects labelled A and B.

Reading and rounding measurements

Learn

The diagram shows the distance of a number of javelin throws.

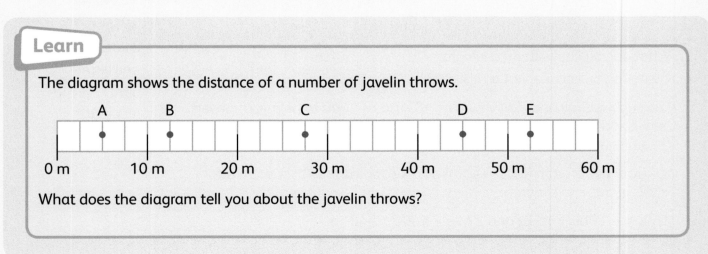

What does the diagram tell you about the javelin throws?

Practise

1 Write the distance of each javelin throw:

   a in metres

   b in centimetres

   c rounded to the nearest ten metres

   d rounded to the nearest metre.

2 Afia throws her javelin further than throw B but not as far as throw C.

   a Which of these distances **cannot** be Afia's throw?

   3 500 cm   23.5 m   2 950 cm   2 200 cm   25.75 m

   b Order these distances from shortest to longest.

3 Draw four lines and measure them accurately.

   Record each length in centimetres and in millilitres.

   Order the lengths from longest to shortest.

   Now round each length to the nearest whole centimetre.

Try this

1 Follow the instructions below, writing a new value when you need to, or keeping the same value if you can.

   How many times did you need to write a new value?

   a Write down a mass that rounds to 2 kg, when rounding to the nearest kg.

   b Write down a mass that is also heavier than 2 250 g.

   c Write down a mass that is also not a multiple of 0.1 kg.

   d Write down a mass that is also a multiple of 25 g.

   e Write down a mass that could be the missing mass when placed in this order:

   2.35 kg, 2 380 g, 2.4 kg, _____, 2 475 g.

Think like a mathematician

Remember to convert between kilograms and grams to help you.

85

7b Length, area and perimeter

Explore

Key words

area
perimeter
polygon
regular
formula
centimetres
squared

Can you compare the lengths of the worms for the wormery?

Finding areas and perimeters

Learn

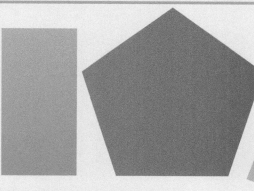

Here is a sequence of regular and irregular shapes.

Carefully measure one side of each regular shape. What do you notice?

Now measure each side of the irregular shapes.

How can you quickly calculate the perimeter of a regular shape?

What happens with an irregular shape?

Can you predict the perimeter of the next regular shape in the sequence?

Practise

1 Calculate the perimeters of these shapes.
   The first one has been done for you.
   a An equilateral triangle with sides of 16 cm
      16 cm × 3 = 48 cm
   b An irregular pentagon with two sides of
      25 cm and three sides of 30 cm.
   c A regular octagon with sides of 18 cm.
   d An irregular hexagon with three sides of
      0.32 m and three sides of 0.18 m.

2 Here is a rectangular flag.

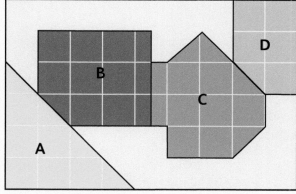

   a What are the areas of the polygons
      A, B, C and D?
   b What is the area of the flag in small
      squares?

Try this

Do you agree with Orlando?

When I use two of these rectangles
to make a larger rectangle, the area
and perimeter are double the size of
this rectangle.

7c Time

What months on a calendar could this be?

Key words

second

minute

hour

day

week

fortnight

analogue clock

digital clock

duration

interval

calendar

timetable

Using units of time

Learn

Analogue clocks have two circular number lines: one for the hours, and one for the minutes. The distance along each number line is shown by the hands.

Digital clocks show the time in digits. The minutes are shown as the number of minutes past the hour. Digital clocks can display according to a 12-hour or 24-hour system. Which system is shown here?

a.m.

What is the difference between the times in minutes?

Practise

1 Here are the times of some programmes on a television channel.

09:45	Garden world
10:35	Cartoons
10:50	Music special
12:00	News
12:20	Film: Jungle Adventure
14:25	Sport focus

a Calculate the length of each programme.

b Sport Focus lasts for 100 minutes. What time does it finish?

2 How many:

a days are there in six weeks

b hours are there in one week

c hours are there in 14 days

d minutes are there in 3.5 hours

e seconds are there in seven minutes?

3 A train journey takes 175 minutes.

It begins before noon and ends after 14:00.

a Find some possible start and end times for the train journey.

b Explain why the train journey does not begin at 11:05.

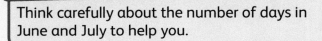

Try this

Orlando meets his friend on Saturday 10 June.

They arrange to meet on four more Saturdays during the next two months.

On which of these dates did they not meet?

8 July

24 June

4 August

22 July

19 August

Think like a mathematician

Think carefully about the number of days in June and July to help you.

⟳ 7d Problem solving

Explore

Key words
height
weight
mass
capacity
centimetres
millimetres
millilitres

'The Crow and the Pitcher' is one of Aesop's Fables.

The story is about a thirsty crow that finds a pitcher with water at the bottom. But the water level is so low that the crow cannot reach it with its beak.

How can the crow reach the water?

Solving problems

Carefully collect some small stones from the garden or the school grounds.

Start with 300 ml of water in a clear plastic container.

Measure the height of the water level.

What mass of stones is needed for the water level to reach the top of the container?

Practise

1 Work with a partner to measure the mass of the stone and the new height of the water level each time.

Record your findings in a table like this.

Stone	0	1	2	3	4	5	6
Mass (g)	0 g	g	g	g	g	g	g
Height of water (cm)							

2 Now answer these questions.

  a By how much did the water level rise after you dropped in the first stone?

  b How much further must the water rise to reach the top of the container?

  c What is the total mass of the first three stones you dropped into the container?

  d How far did the water level rise in total?

Try this

Begin the investigation again, but this time with only 150 ml of water in the container.

Use the same stones as before.

Can you calculate how far the water will rise each time using the results you got before to help you? What calculations will you use to help you?

Think like a mathematician

Remember to use what you know to help you work out how much higher the water will rise. Then check to see if you were correct.

Self-check

A The metric system

1 Convert these measurements to the units shown.
   a 3.45 kg to grams (g)
   b 3 750 ml to litres (ℓ)
   c 1 255 cm to metres (m)
   d 45.2 cm to millimetres (mm)

2 a Put these lengths in order from shortest to longest.

   265 cm   2.4 m   2.25 m   270 cm

   b Now round these lengths to the nearest metre.

3 What are the values of A, B and C on this weighing scale?

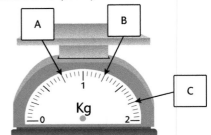

B Length, area and perimeter

1 a Measure only one side of each of these regular polygons and then calculate the perimeter of each.
   b Look at the triangle and the pentagon. What is the approximate area of each shape?

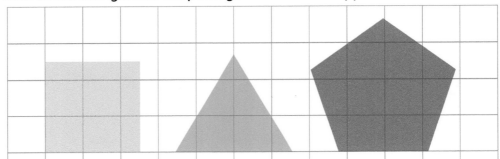

2 The area of a rectangle is 18 cm². What could its dimensions be? Find two possible solutions.

C Time

1 How much later is the time shown on the digital clock?

p.m.

2 Here is part of a bus timetable.

Willow Creek	Brook Park	South Hills	Poppy Springs
14:45	15:07	15:39	16:02

   a How long does the bus take to travel from Willow Creek to Poppy Springs?
   b It is a quarter to three. How long will a passenger need to wait until the next bus from Brook Park?

3 Complete these sentences.
   a Three weeks after 25 April is

   _____.

   b Ten days before 8 January is

   _____.

   c 5 September is _____ days after 8 August. How many weeks is this?

Unit 8 Number and problem solving

8a Number patterns

Explore

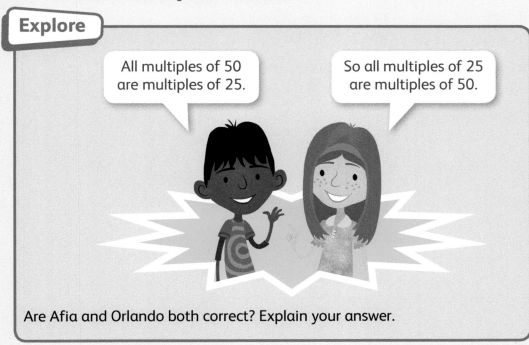

All multiples of 50 are multiples of 25.

So all multiples of 25 are multiples of 50.

Are Afia and Orlando both correct? Explain your answer.

Key words

sequence
rule
term
next
previous
multiple

Finding rules and describing patterns

Learn

Here are the first three terms in a sequence. What is the same and what is different each time?

What will the next term look like? How many straws will there be?
Will a term with 20 straws be in the pattern? How do you know?

The rule for the pattern is **next term equals previous term plus two**, or, **add two**.

> **Practise**

1 a Use the rule for the pattern to work out the number of straws in the following terms:

   5th term   8th term   10th term   15th term

  b Which term will be made of 41 straws?

2 What is the difference in the number of straws between these pairs of terms?

  a 1st and 3rd   b 2nd and 4th   c 2nd and 8th   d 3rd and 9th

  e Find another pair of terms with the same difference as the 2nd and 8th terms.
   What do you notice?

3 Here is the start of some different sequences. Find the rule and the value of the 6th term each time.

  a 5, 9, 13, 17, …   b 15, 10, 5, 0, …

  c 39, 30, 21, …   d 10, 9.4, 8.8, …

  e $5\frac{3}{5}, 5\frac{1}{5}, 4\frac{4}{5}, …$ f $17\frac{1}{4}, 16\frac{1}{2}, 15\frac{3}{4}, …$

Think like a mathematician

If you can find the difference between terms in a sequence, it can help you to find the rule. But check to make sure that the rule continues for all terms.

> **Try this**

What is the rule for this sequence? Work out the 10th term.

Do you need to work out the 9th term first or can you use a different way?

Patterns with multiples

Learn

Look at this pattern made using five cent coins.

What is the value of each row?

What is the value of the top two rows?

What is the value of the top three rows?

What is the value of all the rows?

What do you notice about the totals each time?

The total of all the rows is also a multiple of 25 and of 50.

Practise

1 Write the value of the rows. The first one has been done for you.

   a The 6th row   6th row will have 6 coins so 5c × 6 = 30c.

   b The 7th row

   c The 8th row

   d The total of the first six rows

   e The total of the first eight rows.

2 a How many rows are needed so that the total of all rows is another multiple of 25c?

   b Write down the next total of all rows that is a multiple of 25c.

8b Multiplication and division

Explore

Key words
scale
product
divisible
remainder
inverse
square
multiple
factor

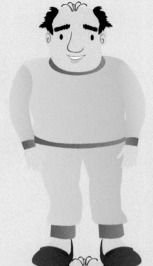

1st   2nd   3rd   4th

Afia has been making a picture using giants of different sizes.

How tall could each giant be?

Using multiplication and division facts

Learn

Multiplication and division are the inverse of each other. This means that you can use multiplication to find division facts and vice versa. You can use division to find multiplication facts.

> I only know my tables up to 10 × 10. What can I do to help me with 75 ÷ 5?

Partitioning can be used to answer difficult calculations.

75 can be partitioned into 50 and 25.

$75 \div 5 = 50 \div 5 + 25 \div 5$

$\qquad = 10 + 5$

$\qquad = 15$

This array shows the inverse using multiplication.

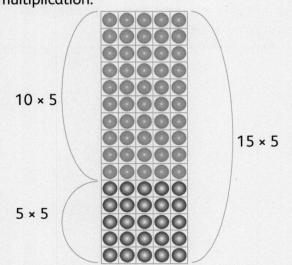

10 × 5

15 × 5

5 × 5

Practise

1   Complete the calculations and give the related division fact each time

  a   6 × 7 =   b   7 × 8 =

  c   8 × 9 =   d   9 × 10 =

  e   ☐ × 7 = 21   f   8 × ☐ = 32

2   Use partitioning to calculate the following:

  a   72 ÷ 6 =   b   78 ÷ 6 =

  c   84 ÷ 7 =   d   96 ÷ 8 =

  e   95 ÷ 5 =   f   91 ÷ 7 =

Check your answers using the inverse.

3   Orlando cuts a 98 cm strip of paper into seven equal strips.

How do you know that the length of each smaller strip is in whole centimetres?

Try this

75	84	49	72	95
56	96	88	93	91
66	80	48	77	57

How many numbers are multiples of 5?

Find all the numbers that are multiples of 6.

Find at least four numbers that are not multiples of 7.

Find all the numbers that are multiples of 8.

Find at least four numbers that are not multiples of 9.

How can you prove that your answers are correct?

Finding factor pairs

Learn

You can also use the multiplication facts to help work out factor pairs.

How do you know that 2, 5 and 10 are definitely factors of 40?

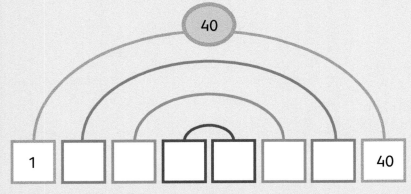

How can you use factor pairs for 40 to help you work out factor pairs for 80?

Practise

1   Find the factor pairs for the following:

   a   20   b   15   c   30

   d   60   e   75

   f   What do you notice about the factor pairs for 15, 30 and 60?

   Are there any patterns?

2   True or false?

   a   19 has 2 pairs of factors.

   b   21 has 2 pairs of factors.

   c   42 has 4 pairs of factors.

   d   25 has only 3 factors.

3   Now find factor pairs for some larger numbers:

   a   72   b   84   c   95

Think like a mathematician

Use partitioning and your multiplication tables to help you, but also think about factors that can and cannot be possible. For example, can an odd number have an even number as a factor?

Using factors to multiply

Learn

We can write 90 × 5 as 9 × 10 × 5 using factors of 90 and reorder this as 9 × 5 × 10.
We can write 900 × 5 as 9 × 100 × 5 using factors of 900 and reorder this as 9 × 5 × 100.

What factors of 90 and 900 were used? Why is this a useful strategy?

Look at the way that factors have been used in this calculation.
We can write 6 × 14 as 6 × 7 × 2.
The calculation can be completed as 42 × 2 or double 42.

Or we can write 6 × 14 as 2 × 3 × 14.
The calculation can be completed as 28 × 3 or 42 × 2.

Practise

1 Rewrite each of these calculations using factors and then solve them.
  Work down the columns. The first one has been done for you.

  a 70 × 6 = 7 × 10 × 6 = 7 × 6 × 10 = 420   b 700 × 6 =   c 6 × 18 =

     70 × 7 =   700 × 7 =   15 × 4 =

     80 × 5 =   800 × 5 =   24 × 4 =

     5 × 40 =   5 × 400 =   9 × 16 =

2 Take one number from the square and two
  operations each time.

  Write them as two different calculations.

  Here is an example:

  15 × 2 × 4 =

  15 × 8 =

  How many different products can you make?

15	23
17	21

  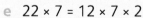

3 True or false?

  a 9 × 6 = 9 × 3 × 2

  b 12 × 9 = 6 × 9 × 3

  c 16 × 4 = 8 × 4 × 2

  d 7 × 8 = 7 × 2 × 2 × 2

  e 22 × 7 = 12 × 7 × 2

Using factors to multiply by 25

Learn

4 and 25 are a factor pair of 100.

You can use the multiplication fact 25 × 4 = 100 to help you to multiply different values by 25.

Look at the first array. It represents 12 × 25.

Now look at the other two arrays. How has each one changed?

25

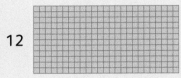
12

50

6

100

3

The area that each array covers is the same, so 12 × 25 = 6 × 50 = 3 × 100.

The number of rows in the last array is equal to 12 ÷ 4.

So 12 × 25 = 12 ÷ 4 × 100 or 12 × 100 ÷ 4.

Practise

1 Calculate the following, using the mental method shown above.

   a 8 × 25   b 25 × 16   c 14 × 25   d 25 × 28   e 0.8 × 25

   f What do you notice about the answers to the first pair of calculations?

      How about the second pair? Can you explain why?

2 Calculate the area of each rectangle.

36 cm

25 cm   A

55 cm  B

25 cm

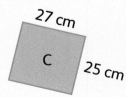
27 cm

C

25 cm

Doubles and halves

Doubling and halving are useful mental strategies.

You can use what you know about doubling and halving two-digit numbers to help you double and halve decimal numbers and multiples of 10 or 100.

Double 34 is 68.
Double 340 is 680.
Double 3 400 is 6 800.
Double 3.4 is 6.8.
What do you notice?

Now halve each of these numbers.
What do you notice?

Practise

1 a Double each of these numbers. Work down the columns.

48	55	76
480	550	760
4 800	5 500	7 600
4.8	5.5	7.6
0.48	0.55	0.76

   b Halve the first three numbers in each column.

   c Now use what you know to halve the decimal numbers 4.8, 5.5, 7.6 and 0.48.

2 Write the two missing lengths each time.

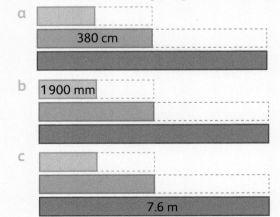

   a 380 cm

   b 1900 mm

   c 7.6 m

Try this

I am thinking of a three-digit multiple of 10 that is not a multiple of 100. I double it and double it again.

I am thinking of a multiple of 100. I halve it and halve it again.

Both learners get the same answer.
Explore to find a possible starting number for each learner.

Think like a mathematician

Try doubling some three-digit multiples of ten. What do you notice about the answers each time? What happens when you halve multiples of 100? How can this help you?

Using rounding and adjusting to multiply

You have used rounding and adjusting to add and subtract near multiples of 10 and 100. You can use a similar strategy to help you multiply.

How much will it cost to buy 5 copies of each game?

Each game costs approximately $20 so you can use $20 × 5 = $100 to help you. What must you do next?

Start with the $19 game. Is $100 too much money or not enough? Why? Is $100 too much or not enough for the game that costs $21?

You can write calculations to help you keep track of the process.

$$\$19 \times 5 = (\$20 \times 5) - (\$1 \times 5)$$
$$= \$100 - \$5$$
$$= \$95$$

This array also shows that 19 x 5 is 5 less than 20 x 5.

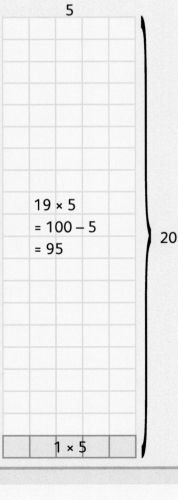

5

19 × 5
= 100 − 5
= 95

19

20

1   1 × 5

Practise

1 Find the total costs for the number of
Buzz Beetle games each time.

Write a calculation to help you keep track.

a 8 copies

b 4 copies

c 12 copies

d 9 copies.

2 Find the total costs for the number of
Cool Carz games each time.

Write a calculation to help you keep track.

a 8 copies

b 4 copies

c 12 copies

d 9 copies

Try this

1 Calculate the perimeter of these
regular shapes that each have sides
of 19 cm.

2 How much longer will each perimeter
be if all sides are 21 cm?

Work out a rule using what you
already know. Do this instead of
calculating the perimeters again.

Applying methods of multiplication and division

Learn

Afia and Orlando make a board game.

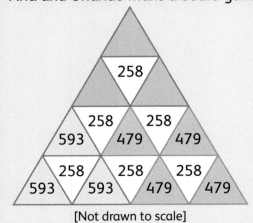

[Not drawn to scale]

Which colour triangles – white, green or
yellow – will have the largest total? Estimate
first and explain your thinking. Why will a
written method be more useful to calculate
the actual totals?

The blue triangles have a total value of 852.
What is the value of one blue triangle?

The children use 16 triangles in total.
Each has an area of 35 cm².
What is the total area of the board game?

103

Practise

1 Write these calculations. Make an estimate each time. Work down the columns.

347 × 6	357 × 6	457 × 6
348 × 7	358 × 7	458 × 7
349 × 8	359 × 8	459 × 8
3.4 × 6	5.7 × 7	4.5 × 8

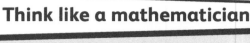

Think like a mathematician

You can use what you know about multiplying whole numbers to multiply decimals. As 34 × 6 = 204, then 3.4 × 6 must be ten times smaller.
You can also partition 3.4 into 3 and 0.4 to calculate 3.4 × 6 as 3 × 6 add 0.4 × 6, using what you know about 4 × 6 to help you multiply 0.4 × 6

2 a Calculate the mass of each shape on the weighing scales. Check your answers using the inverse.

744 g 651 g 560 g

b Use what you know about the mass of one yellow shape in 2a to find the total mass of each set of shapes below.

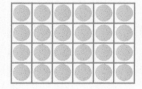  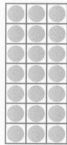

3 Find the missing digits in each of these calculations.

a
```
      T  U
      4  □
   ×  3  8
   ─────────
      □  6
   3  2  0
   2  1  0
 1 2  0  0
─────────
 1 7  □  6
```

b
```
      5 □ r 1
   ─────────
 9 │ □ 7 8
```

c
```
      H  T  U
      □  8  7
   ×        □
   ─────────
   3  □  2  2
```

Solving problems

Learn

248 school learners get into groups of an equal size for sports day.
There are 3 learners left without a group.
How did they group themselves?

Now 248 learners make equal groups in a different way.
This time 5 learners are left without a group.
How did they group themselves?

Practise

1 How many of the 248 learners will be left out each time? The first one has been done for you.

   a When they make groups of six

   > 248 ÷ 6 = 41 r 3, so 3 learners will be left out of a group.

   b When they make groups of ten

   c When they make groups of seven

   d When they make groups of eight.

2 The learners are in groups of eight. Each group collects a bucket of 25 balls.

   How many balls are there in total?

3 The school buys balls in boxes of 100. Each box costs $39.

   How much money did the school spend in total so they had enough balls for sports day? Remember that you already know the total number of balls from question 2.

4 At the refreshment stop, all the learners have one cup of either lemon or orange drink.

   The lemon drink is in 165 ml cups.
   The orange drink is in 180 ml cups.

   | 165 ml | 180 ml |

   Find all the possible total amounts of drink that a group of 8 learners can have at the refreshment stop. Give all solutions in millilitres (ml).

Think like a mathematician

Try to be systematic with your investigation so that you do not miss out any solutions. Perhaps start by thinking about the learners all having the same kind of drink.

Try this

In my group of 8, we took double the amount of millilitres of orange drink as lemon drink.

Is this possible? Prove your thinking.

Self-check

A Number patterns

1 a The first term in a sequence is 85. The rule is **subtract seven**.
Write the next five terms in the sequence.

  b Multiples of 25 are always odd.
Do you agree with this statement? Why?

2 Find the rule and the missing numbers in these sequences each time.

  a ___, 6, 3, ___, ___, ___, −9

  b −50, ___, ___, 25, 50, 75

  c 40, 110, ___, ___, 320, 390, ___

  d $1\frac{3}{4}$, $1\frac{1}{4}$, ___, ___, $-\frac{1}{4}$, ___

B Multiplication and division

1 What is a good estimate for these calculations?
Will the actual answers be smaller or larger each time?

  a 387 × 9   b 75 × 47   c 594 ÷ 3   d 658 ÷ 9

  e Now complete the calculations using a method of your choice.
How close were your estimates?

2 Use multiplication facts and place value to calculate:

  a 3.6 × 3
  b 5.2 × 4
  c 4.8 × 5
  d 7.4 × 6

3 Use factors to help you complete these calculations.

  a 14 × 5   b 7 × 18   c 20 × 17

4 36.2   42.56   64.5   18.45

  a Double the blue numbers.
  b Halve the green numbers.

9a Organising, categorising and representing data

Explore

Do you think more people use the trains on weekdays than at the weekend?

Will this pattern be the same throughout the year?

How can you find information to help answer these questions?

Key words

data

discrete

represent

mode

discrete data

continuous data

Representing data

Learn

Data is information. We can represent data in many ways. The way we represent (show) the data will allow us to show a lot of information in a small space that can be easily understood and used.

The way we represent the data will depend on the type of data that has been collected and how it needs to be used.

Pictograms, frequency tables and bar charts are used to represent discrete data. Discrete data is data that can be counted; for example, the number of people or the number of cars.

What does the data in the bar chart tell you?

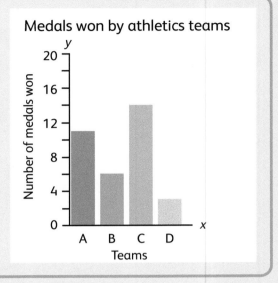

Medals won by athletics teams

Practise

1   Nine people did not take part in any of these weekend activities.

    How would you show this information on the pictogram?

2   Use the representation to compare the data.

    Describe three different things that the data tells you.

Weekend activities

Outside games

Walking

Swimming

Meeting friends

Other

Try this

Look at the bar chart about the medals.

Afia and Orlando each draw their own bar chart to show this information. Orlando uses a scale so that every 1 cm shows a step of 5. Afia uses a scale so that every 1 cm shows a step of 2.

Draw Afia's bar chart.

Explain why the length of the bars on Afia's chart will be longer than on Orlando's chart.

Key

represents 4 people

Collecting, organising and representing data

Learn

We collect data to answer questions, but it is important that this information helps you to find out what you want to know. For example, there is no point in collecting information about people's heights when you want to find out about their favourite subjects at school!

It is easier to spot and compare patterns when data is organised.
Here is a frequency table showing favourite subjects.
The value 18 occurs most often in this set of data. This is called the mode.

Subject	Mathematics	English	Science	Sport	Art	Other
Frequency	25	18	24	26	18	9

The data should allow you to find out what you want to know, but you may also need to ask other questions and collect more data.
What other questions would you want to ask?

Practise

1 a Use the information about favourite subjects and represent the data using a pictogram or bar chart. If you use a bar chart, label the y-axis in 5s so that it reads 0, 5, 10, 15, and so on.

   b Make up two different questions to ask about your chart.

2 How will you investigate the following question?
   How will you collect and organise your data?

   Most words in the English language contain at least one of the vowels a, e, i, o, u. Therefore, is it true that you will find more vowels than any other letter in the alphabet in a page of a book?

   a What is the mode of your data set?

   b Choose a way to represent your findings for the five letters that appear most often.

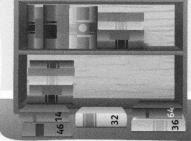

Line graphs

Learn

We use **line graphs** to represent continuous data, particularly data about change over a period of time. This is data that is measured and has a continuous scale, for example, height or volume.

Here are two different line graphs. Look at the value for Day 6 on the graph about rainwater and the value for 11:30 a.m. on the graph about the skate-park. What do you notice about the values? Do they both make sense?

Rainwater collected in a container

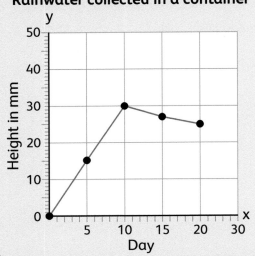

Visitors to skate-park

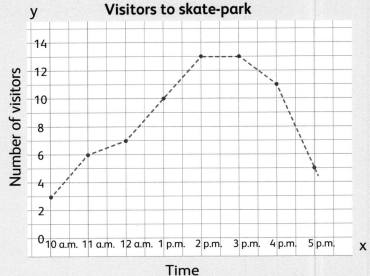

Practise

1 Use the line graph about rainwater to answer these questions.

 a How many millimetres of rainwater were recorded on Day 5?

 b How many more millimetres of rainwater were recorded on Day 20?

 c On which days was rainwater recorded at more than 2.5 cm?

 d What is a good estimate for the rainfall recorded on Day 12?

2 Represent the following information about maximum temperature in a line graph. Choose an appropriate scale and labels for your line graph.

Day	1	2	3	4	5	6
Temp °C	17	23	15	9	20	26

3 How will you investigate the following question? How will you collect and organise your data?

 How does my heart rate change with exercise?

 a Collect and organise data about heart rate and exercise.

  What decisions will you need to make?

 b Represent the data on a line graph.

  Use the x-axis for time and the y-axis for your heart rate. Remember to think about a sensible scale for your x-axis so that you can clearly show the measurements.

 c How can the data help you to answer the original question?

9b Probability

Explore

Key words 🔄

probability
impossible
unlikely
likely
equally likely
even chance
certain

I think I will be able to swim around the coastline in 24 hours!

The language of probability is used to show how likely or unlikely events might be.

Do you think these events are likely or unlikely to happen, or are they impossible? Why?

Using the language of probability

Learn

Look at the language of probability used here to show how likely it is for someone to pick a green ball from the bag.

impossible   unlikely   equally likely   likely   certain

Practise

1   Describe the probability of these events.

   a   Spinning an odd number

   b   Spinning a number greater than 6

   c   Spinning a number less than 6

   d   Using two spinners and spinning a total of one

   e   Using two spinners and spinning a total greater than one.

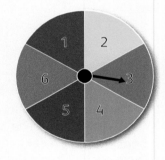

2   Orlando has these coins in his money box.
   One coin falls out.

   Use the language of probability to
   say whether:

   a   a 5c coin falls out

   b   a 5c coin does not fall out

   c   a 25c coin falls out

   d   a coin that represents an even number of
       cents falls out

   e   a coin that is not worth 10c falls out.

3

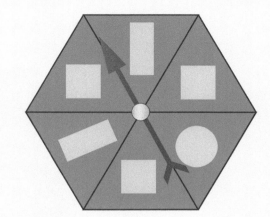

A   B

What are the missing probability words?

a You are _____ to spin a square on spinner B.

b It is _____ to spin a pentagon on spinner B.

c You are _____ to spin a square on spinner A.

Try this

Draw or make your own two spinners.

Decide what you will put on each one so that you can make up some missing word sentences about them.

Can you make up a set of sentences so that a friend has to use each of the probability words at least once?

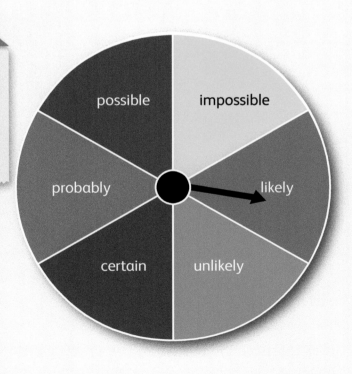

9c Problem solving

Explore

Key words
table
list
systematic

If all **these** friends play each other once, how many games of badminton will be played in total?

Using tables and lists

Learn

Tables and lists can be used to organise information, making it easier to spot patterns or find missing information.

The following table shows the number of games won or lost by the badminton players this year, but some of the data is missing.

Write the missing information in the table.

Games	Person 1	Person 2	Person 3	Total
Games won	17	15		
Games lost			18	47
Total games played	31		32	

Practise

1 Write the missing information in the following table about the number of visitors to a sports club:

a At 10:00 a.m. on Saturday

b At 12:00 p.m. across all days

c At 2:00 p.m. on Friday.

	10:00 a.m.	12:00 p.m.	2:00 p.m.
Friday	125	200	
Saturday		275	350
Sunday	180	325	410
Total	450		1 000

2 Sunday is a busy day at the sports club.

By 2:30 p.m., 120 more people have arrived at the club but 45 people have left.

The same pattern continues every 30 minutes until 6:30 p.m.

a How many people are in the club at 6:30 p.m.?

You can use a list like this to help solve the problem.

Time	Arrive	Leave	Total

b What if the pattern changes from 6:30 p.m. until 9 p.m. so that the number of people that arrive at the club every 30 minutes is now half the number that leave?

Explore this new pattern and find a set of examples that work.

Try this

Use the information below to make a table to find out:

- which friends (A, B and C) can meet for coffee each day
- which two friends (A and B, A and C, or B and C) cannot meet for coffee that week?

Friend A can meet for coffee on Monday, Tuesday and Thursday.
Friend B cannot meet for coffee on Tuesday.
All three friends cannot meet together on any of the days.
Friend C always meets the same friend for coffee on two days.

Working systematically to solve problems

Learn

Using a systematic approach will help to solve problems.

You can be systematic by using order, for example, trying numbers in the order 1, 2, 3, 4, 5 rather than 2, 4, 1, 5, 3.

You can be systematic by keeping one thing the same and seeing how many solutions you can find, and then changing to keep a different thing the same. An example of this approach is the 'How many different badminton games can be played?' problem on page 114.

Practise

1 What if you double a number and then divide it by four? Is the answer always a whole number?

   a Explore this idea with your own examples. Use a list to organise your results.

   b Make up your own 'What if' questions to explore this statement. Be ready to share what you have found out.

2 Here is a set of numbers: 10, 20, 30, 40, 50

   a How many different totals can you make by adding pairs of these numbers?

   b What if the rule is **adding three numbers** to make different totals?
      Will there be more or fewer solutions?

Try this

I can only choose two of these toys to play with at a time. How many different choices do I have?

Think like a mathematician

Always read a problem carefully. This one asks you to find 'different totals' so remember to look out for totals that are the same and do not include them in your results.

Try to use a systematic approach to solve Afia's problem.

What if there are two identical spinning tops?

How does this change the number of different choices that Afia has?

Now make up your own 'What if …?' question to explore.

Be ready to share what you have found out.

Self-check

A Collecting, organising and representing data

1 What is the mode of this set of numbers?
19, 17, 20, 8, 17, 8, 15, 17, 10

2 Here is a frequency table about the children in Afia and Orlando's class. It shows how many children have a different number of brothers and sisters.

Number of brothers and sisters	0	1	2	3	4
Frequency	3	8	12	4	3

a How many children are in the class altogether?
b How many children had more than two brothers and sisters?
c How many more children had two brothers and sisters than no brothers and sisters?

3 Look at the rainfall line graph on page 110.
On day 25 (not shown), the amount of rainfall recorded was 18 mm.
How much more rainfall was recorded on Day 15 than on Day 25?

B Probability

1 What is the probability of turning over an even number from a set of face-down cards numbered 1 to 10?

2 What is the probability of turning over a multiple of 10 from a set of face-down cards numbered 1 to 100?

3 What is the probability of turning over a multiple of 100 from a set of face-down cards numbered 25 to 30?

4 What is the probability of turning over a two-digit number from a set of face-down cards numbered 30 to 50?

Unit 10 Problem solving and review

10a Problem solving

Explore

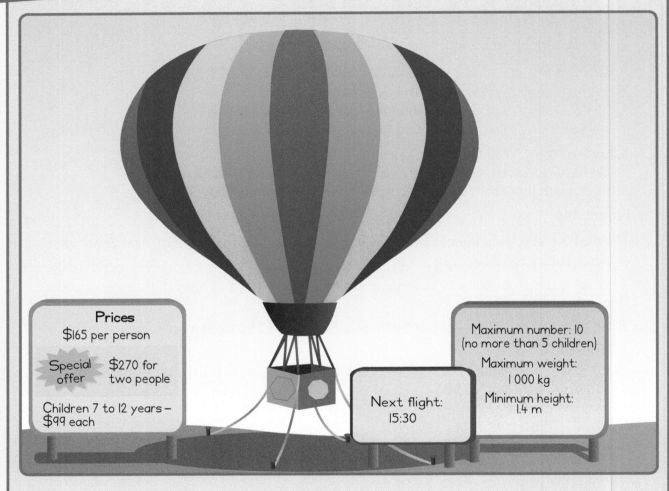

Prices
$165 per person

Special offer $270 for two people

Children 7 to 12 years – $99 each

Next flight: 15:30

Maximum number: 10 (no more than 5 children)

Maximum weight: 1 000 kg

Minimum height: 1.4 m

All the problems in this unit are about a hot air balloon ride.

Look at all the information here. Can you think of any word problems about the hot air balloon ride?

What do I know?

1 What is the price of a hot air balloon ride for:

   a a family with two adults and two children

   b five individual people

   c two couples?

3 Three people arrive for the balloon ride at the following times:

   How long must each person wait for the balloon ride?

2 How will you prove your answers to these questions:

   a What is the most money that the balloon company can earn for one ride?

   b How much more is this than the least amount of money that the company can earn for one ride?

p.m.

Making decisions

Person	A	B	C	D	E	F	G	H	I	J	K	L	M	N
Weight in kg	40	61	99	65	85	120	101	45	115	80	95	105	75	125

1 a What is the height of each person?

   b Who is not tall enough for the balloon ride?

   c About how much taller is person F than person E?

   d What fraction of this group is more than 1.7 m tall?

2 Child H is tall enough to go on the balloon ride, but she is the youngest person in the group. The balloon ride is exactly 1100 days after her 4th birthday.
Is she old enough to go on the ride?

3 a Can any ten people taller than 1.4 m go on a balloon ride together? Why or why not?

   You can make estimates to help you calculate.

   b What if each person takes a bag weighing 10 kg? Can any ten people still go?

Solving different problems

1 Here is a timetable for balloon rides for part of a year.

Time of year	Morning	Afternoon
March	07:00	15:30
April	07:00	17:00
May	06:30	17:30
June	06:00	18:30

a It is 15 March. How many days will people have to wait before the 5 o'clock in the afternoon ride starts?

b There are no rides in December, January and February.

How many days will people have to wait between the last ride on 30 November and the first ride on 1 March?

c How does this number of days change for a leap year?

2 The main part of the basket holds 10 people.
Each person (P) can stand in a different section.

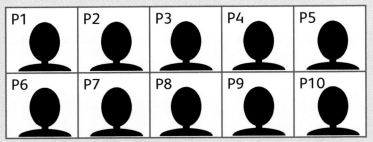

a Five people: P1, P2, P3, P4 and P5 line up to choose their place in the first row of the basket.

Investigate to find the different ways that the five people could have arranged themselves in the first row, for example P1, P2, P5, P3, P4.

b The mass of the five people in the second row is exactly 499 kg. They have no bags.
Use the information from before to work out which five people this could be.
Is there more than one solution?

c Is it possible for the mass of all ten people to be exactly 1000 kg?
Show your thinking.

3

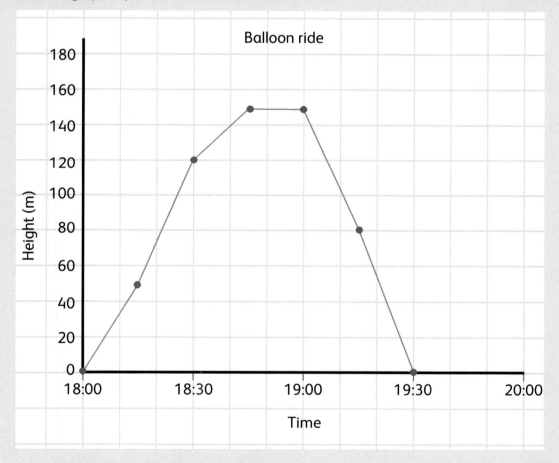

These regular shapes are used as landing zones for the hot air balloon.

These shapes are all different so they can never have the same perimeter length.

Explore the statement with your own examples to find out if this is always, sometimes or never true.

4 The line graph represents the hot air balloon ride.

a Use what you already know to decide which time of year this balloon ride could have taken place.

b How high was the balloon 15 minutes after take-off?

c For approximately how many minutes was the balloon above 80 metres?

d The balloon was at a height of 150 m for exactly $\frac{1}{6}$ of the ride.
Is this statement true? How do you know?

⟳ 11a Rounding and ordering

Explore

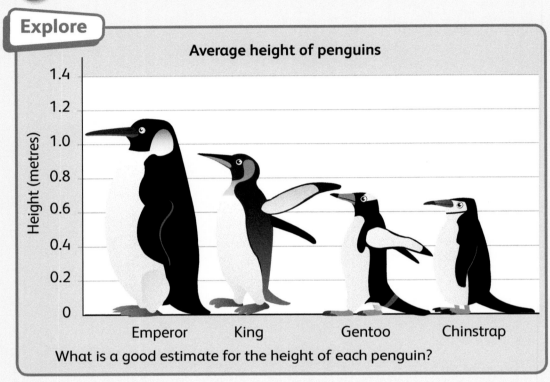

Average height of penguins

What is a good estimate for the height of each penguin?

Key words

tenths
hundredths
greater than
less than
negative
positive
temperature
Celsius

Ordering and comparing decimal numbers

Learn

How do these different representations prove that Afia is wrong?

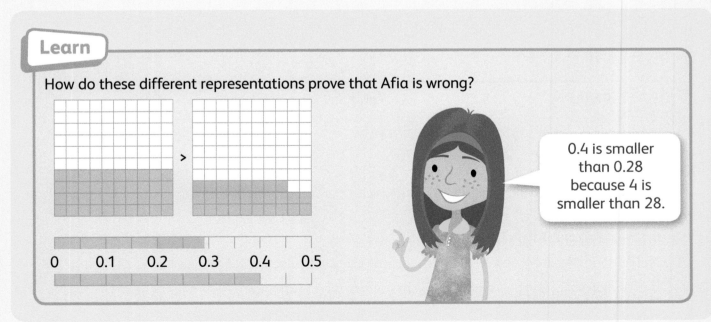

0.4 is smaller than 0.28 because 4 is smaller than 28.

Practise

1 Compare the following decimal numbers.

Use the symbols < or = or > each time. The first one has been done for you.

a 3.4 and 3.04   3.4 is greater than 3.04 so 3.4 > 3.04

b 3.4 and 3.40   c 3.8 and 3.68

d 3.80 and 3.86   e 4.8 and 4.86   f 5.9 and 6.09

2 The average heights of different species of penguins are shown here.

Adélie	Chinstrap	King	Emperor	Gentoo
0.7 m	0.68 m	0.95 m	1.15 m	0.71 m

a How many times larger are the values of each digit 1 in 1.15 m than the digit 1 in 0.71 m?

b Write the heights of the penguins in order from tallest to shortest.

c What measurement is exactly halfway between 0.95 m and 1.15 m on a number line?

Try this

Use each digit only once to make this statement true.
Is there more than one solution?   1   5   4   6

4.☐5 > ☐.5☐ > 4.☐

Rounding decimal numbers

Learn

You can also use place value to help round decimal numbers.

Look again at the average heights of the different species of penguins.

All measurements round to the same whole metre, but do they all round to the same tenth of a whole metre?

Use the number line representation to prove why the heights of the Chinstrap and Gentoo penguins round to the same tenth of a whole metre.

Practise

1 Write five different measurements each time that round to the following measurements.

   a 7 m

   b 7.1 m

   c 6.9 m

   d 10 m

2 Here are the recorded masses of some different penguins.

Adélie	Chinstrap	King	Emperor	Gentoo
4.9 kg	4.49 kg	13.8 kg	22.45 kg	5.21 kg

   a Round each mass to the nearest whole kilogram (kg).

   b Round each mass to the nearest 0.1 kg.

3 Orlando writes down a decimal number.

   It rounds to 3.

   He adds $\frac{3}{10}$ to his number.

   It now rounds to 4.

   Find some different numbers that Orlando could have written down.

Ordering and comparing positive and negative numbers

Learn

Remember that positive numbers are greater than zero and negative numbers are less than zero.

Think of a pair of positive and negative numbers that are both the same distance from zero.

How can you prove this?

You can compare and order positive and negative numbers using the symbols < and >.

$$-8 \quad -6 \quad -4 \quad -2 \quad 0 \quad 2 \quad 4 \quad 6 \quad 8$$

−4 is less than 2 so you write −4 < 2.

But −7 is less than −4, so the order of all three numbers can be shown as −7 < −4 < 2.

Practise

1 Now use the same number line to answer these questions.

   a Which number is three less than zero?

   b Which whole number is between −2 and −4?

   c Which number is four less than one?

   d Which positive number is the same distance from zero as −5?

2 Which is larger? Use the correct symbol each time to show your answer.

   a −12 and −13   b 0 and −1

   c 4 and −4   d −5 and −15

3 True or false? Work down the columns.

3 > 0 > −4	−10 < 2 < −6	−15 < −20 < −5
−4 < 0 < 3	2 > −6 > −10	−5 > −15 > −20
−4 < 3 < 0	−10 < −6 < −2	−20 < −5 < −15

Think like a mathematician

Remember that the value of negative numbers gets smaller the further they are away from zero.

Calculating a fall or rise in temperature

Learn

The table shows the average temperatures for December in different cities.

	Beijing	Moscow	Anchorage	Munich
High °C	3°C	−4°C	−4°C	4°C
Low °C	−7°C	−9°C	−10°C	−2°C

The highest average temperature in Moscow is 7° lower than the highest average temperature in Beijing. We can check this using a number line.

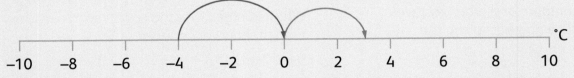

Remember that when a calculation crosses zero, it is useful to stop at zero first before counting on or back.

Practise

1 Answer these questions. The first one has been done for you.

   a How much warmer is the average low temperature for Munich than the average low temperature for Anchorage?

   b What is the difference between the average low and the average high temperature for Beijing?

   c The average low temperature in Moscow is 7° colder than for _____.

   d What is the midway temperature between the high and low values for Anchorage?

   e Which city's average temperatures have a difference of 5°?

2 The thermometer shows the starting temperature each time.

   For each temperature, write the new temperature after:

   a a rise of 12°

   b a fall of 8°

   c a rise of 10°

   d a fall of 12°

   e a fall of 7° followed by a fall of 5°

   f a fall of 11° followed by a rise of 10°.

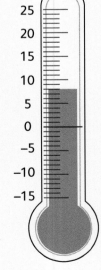

11b Fractions

Explore

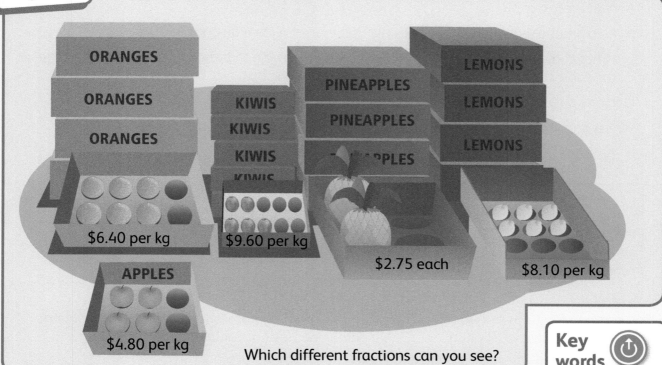

ORANGES
ORANGES
ORANGES

$6.40 per kg

KIWIS
KIWIS
KIWIS
KIWIS

$9.60 per kg

PINEAPPLES
PINEAPPLES
PINEAPPLES

$2.75 each

LEMONS
LEMONS
LEMONS

$8.10 per kg

APPLES

$4.80 per kg

Which different fractions can you see?

Equivalent fractions

Learn

Explain how you know that Afia is correct.

The fractions $\frac{2}{4}$ and $\frac{5}{10}$ are **equivalent**. They share the same position on the number line and represent the same proportion of the whole.

Equivalent fractions have the same value but may not look the same.

The fraction of pineapples left in the box is equal to the fraction of kiwis left in the box.

0   $\frac{1}{10}$ $\frac{2}{10}$ $\frac{3}{10}$ $\frac{4}{10}$ $\frac{5}{10}$ $\frac{6}{10}$ $\frac{7}{10}$ $\frac{8}{10}$ $\frac{9}{10}$ $\frac{10}{10}$

0        $\frac{1}{4}$ $\frac{2}{4}$ $\frac{3}{4}$ $\frac{4}{4}$

1

Key words

tenth
hundredth
fraction
numerator
denominator
equivalent
division
quantity
mixed number
improper fraction
decimal
percentage
ratio
proportion

Practise

1 Answer these questions.

    a Find another pair of fractions from the fruit market picture on page 127 that are equivalent.

    b Limes come in boxes of 12. Quickly sketch a box showing that the number of limes left that is the same fraction as the fraction of oranges left in the box.

2 Odd one out.

    Which fraction is the odd one out each time and is not equivalent to the other two?

    a $\frac{2}{4}$, $\frac{1}{2}$ and $\frac{6}{14}$ b $\frac{1}{3}$, $\frac{4}{9}$ and $\frac{4}{12}$ c $\frac{9}{12}$, $\frac{3}{4}$ and $\frac{7}{8}$ d $\frac{2}{3}$, $\frac{3}{5}$ and $\frac{6}{10}$ e $\frac{4}{6}$, $\frac{2}{3}$ and $\frac{7}{12}$

Fractions of quantities

Learn

You can find fractions of quantities using your understanding of division.

It is useful to find the value of one equal part by dividing the whole by the denominator.

You can then scale up to find the fraction of the whole that you need.

The diagram shows us the cost of different fractions of a kilogram of apples.

1 kg apples = $4.80							
$\frac{1}{8}$	$\frac{1}{8}$	$\frac{1}{8}$	$\frac{1}{8}$	$\frac{1}{8}$	$\frac{1}{8}$	$\frac{1}{8}$	$\frac{1}{8}$
60c	60c	60c	60c	60c	60c	60c	60c

Practise

1 Use the fruit market prices on page 127 to find the cost of:

    a $\frac{1}{2}$ kg of oranges   b $\frac{3}{4}$ kg of apples   c $\frac{1}{10}$ kg of kiwis

    d $\frac{3}{8}$ kg of kiwis   e 500 g of lemons   f 750 g of oranges.

2 The table shows the fraction of customers who bought different fruit from the market on Saturday. There were a total of 360 customers that day.

Apples	Oranges	Kiwis	Pineapples	Lemons	Limes
$\frac{3}{4}$	$\frac{1}{3}$	$\frac{1}{6}$	$\frac{2}{9}$	$\frac{3}{10}$	$\frac{2}{5}$

How many customers bought each type of fruit?

Try this

$\frac{3}{4}$ is greater than $\frac{1}{2}$.

Is this always true, sometimes true, or never true?

Prove your thinking.

More about equivalence

Learn

I bought $\frac{1}{5}$ kg of apples, 0.3 kg of oranges and $\frac{1}{4}$ kg of lemons. Which is the lightest?

I bought $\frac{6}{5}$ kg of kiwis, $1\frac{1}{2}$ kg of apples and $\frac{7}{4}$ kg of oranges. Which is the heaviest?

This diagram represents Afia's oranges.

The fraction $\frac{7}{4}$ is called an improper fraction because the numerator is larger than the denominator. You can say that $\frac{7}{4}$ kg is equal to $\frac{4}{4}$ kg + $\frac{3}{4}$ kg or 1 kg + $\frac{3}{4}$ kg.

This can be written using mixed numbers as $1\frac{3}{4}$ kg. A mixed number has a whole number part and a fraction part.

$\frac{1}{4}$	$\frac{1}{4}$	$\frac{1}{4}$	$\frac{1}{4}$	$\frac{1}{4}$	$\frac{1}{4}$	$\frac{1}{4}$	$\frac{1}{4}$

0 kg   1 kg   2 kg

Practise

1 Order each set of numbers from smallest to largest.

  a $\frac{1}{5}$, 0.1, $\frac{1}{2}$ b 0.75, $\frac{7}{10}$, 0.9   c $\frac{3}{5}$, 0.8, $\frac{2}{8}$ d 0.4, $\frac{1}{3}$, $\frac{2}{5}$

  e 0.2 < ☐ < 0.5. The missing value is a fraction. What could it be?

2 Write the mixed number and improper fraction represented by each diagram.

  a

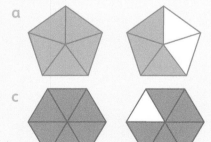

  b

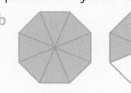

  c

  d

3 Copy this number line. Place the mixed numbers from question 2 on the number line.

0   1   2   3

Introducing percentages

Learn

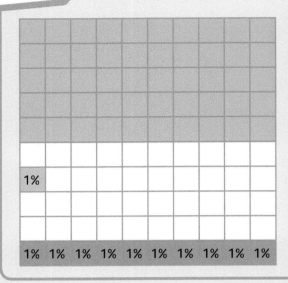

1%

1% 1% 1% 1% 1% 1% 1% 1% 1% 1%

The whole is divided into 100 equal pieces called hundredths.

The word 'percent' means per hundred. One percent (1%) is equal to $\frac{1}{100}$.

We can see that 10% covers $\frac{1}{10}$ of the whole.

What is the fraction and percentage of the whole that is shaded blue?

Knowing these equivalents makes it easier to find percentages of amounts.

Finding 50% is the same as finding $\frac{1}{2}$.

Finding 10% is the same as finding $\frac{1}{10}$ so finding 20% is equal to 10% multiplied by 2.

Practise

1 Write each of the percentages as a fraction with a denominator 100.

  a 50%   b 25%   c 99%

  d 5%   e 75%

  f Which percentage above is equivalent to $\frac{1}{4}$?

  g Which percentage above is equivalent to $\frac{3}{4}$?

2 Find the percentage of each amount of money.

  a 50% of $60   b 25% of $60

  c 75% of $60   d 10% of $80

  e 20% of $80   f 10% of $160

Try this

I am thinking of a percentage. It is larger than $\frac{1}{4}$ but smaller than $\frac{1}{2}$. When I find this percentage of 200 litres, my answer is 60 litres.

What percentage is Orlando thinking of?

Think like a mathematician

Remember to use what you know about finding fractions of amounts. For example, find $\frac{1}{10}$ by dividing by 10.

Proportion

Learn

Like fractions, we can use proportion to compare a part to the whole.

In this group, six out of the ten fruits are oranges.

Proportions are shown as fractions, so the proportion of oranges in this group is $\frac{6}{10}$ or, using what you know about equivalence, $\frac{3}{5}$.

What proportion of the group is apples?

Practise

1 Here are some boxes of fruit.

   a Write the proportion of apples each time.

   b Now write the proportion of bananas each time.

2 The table shows the spelling test results for a group of six children.

Child 1	Child 2	Child 3	Child 4	Child 5	Child 6
12	14	15	10	16	11

   a What proportion of the group scored less than 13 in the test?

   b What proportion of the group scored more than 13 in the test?

   c There are a total of 20 spellings in the test.

      i Write each child's score as a proportion of the whole test.

      ii Can you write any of these scores as equivalent fractions?

3 The proportion of nine year-old boys in a class of 30 is $\frac{1}{5}$.

   There are 9 girls who are nine years old in the same class.

   What proportion of the class is made up of children who are not nine years old?

Think like a mathematician

Remember that there are 30 children in the whole group.
Can you write $\frac{1}{5}$ as a fraction with denominator 30? What is $\frac{1}{5}$ of 30?

Solving problems using ratio

Learn

Ratio is a way of comparing two quantities.
You can use the language 'for every' to talk about ratio.

In this group of fruits, there are 6 oranges
for every 4 apples.

How many apples will there be in two of these groups?
And in three groups? In half a group?

You can use multiplication and division to help find
the relationship between two quantities.

Practise

1   The market stall keeper also sells boxes
of mixed citrus fruits.

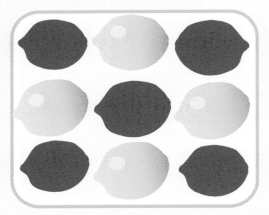

a   Draw a table to record the number of
lemons and limes in:

i   one box

ii   two boxes

iii   three boxes

iv   five boxes

v   ten boxes.

2   Here are the ingredients for a fruit salad
for 6 people.

Fruit salad

3 apples
2 oranges
16 strawberries
1 banana
250 ml fruit juice

a   Write the ingredients for 12 people.

b   Now write the ingredients for 3 people.

c   How many apples are needed for 2 people?

d   How many oranges are needed for 18 people?

11c Addition and subtraction

Explore

10

What could be the value of the yellow part of the bar?
What value would this make the blue part of the bar?

Key words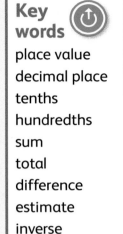

place value

decimal place

tenths

hundredths

sum

total

difference

estimate

inverse

Solving problems using mental and written methods

Learn

I am thinking of 2 three-digit near multiples of 100. The difference between them is 407. When I use rounding to the nearest 100 to add my two numbers, I have to adjust the answer by 2.

What can Afia's numbers be?

Practise

1 Use rounding and adjusting to calculate these additions and subtractions.

Remember to make an estimate first.
Will the actual answer be more or less than your estimate each time?

a 475 + 297 =   b 475 – 297 =

c 799 + 450 =   d 799 – 450 =

e 397 + 249 =   f 249 – 97 =

2 The diagram shows that the difference between two near multiples of 100 is 209.

209

a Find three different pairs of numbers that have this difference.

b Use the inverse each time to check that each pair is possible.

3 Orlando buys several items at the local shop.

He pays with a $5 bill and gets less than $2 in change.

Lolly 75c

Badge 32c

Pencil 69c

Comic 99c

Stickers 85c

a Which combination of items could he buy?

b Which combination of items could he not buy? Why?

Try this

The difference between each pair of vertical boxes is 208.

The sum of each row of four boxes is the same.

Arrange all the numbers to make this true.

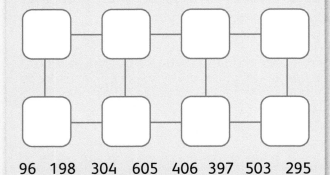

96   198   304   605   406   397   503   295

Think like a mathematician

Think about how you can break the problem down to help you.
You may find it useful to find pairs of numbers with a difference of 208 first.

Adding and subtracting larger numbers and decimals

Learn

Here are the dimensions of three different shapes.

264.5 mm   325.7 mm   583.6 mm

[Not drawn to scale]

What are the missing lengths?

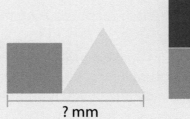

? mm   ? mm

Practise

1. Find the missing lengths each time. Remember to make an estimate first.

a

? mm

b
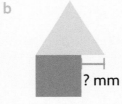
? mm

c
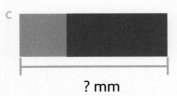
? mm

d
? mm

e. Now check each of your calculations using the inverse.

2. Calculate the following:

a 45.64 + 23.11 =   b 532.4 + 393.3 =   c 408.6 + 315.7 =

d 45.64 − 23.11 =   e 532.4 − 393.3 =   f 408.6 − 315.7 =

3. The table shows the money raised by two charities in different ways.
   Find the missing values.

	Car wash	Sponsored walk	Fair	Exhibition
Charity A	$75.80	$47.68		$48.84
Charity B	$98.75		$48.05	$37.51
Total		$55.35	$84.77	

135

Self-check

A Rounding and ordering

1 a What is the value of the digit 5 in each of these numbers?
  b Order the numbers from smallest to largest.
  c Round each number to the nearest whole number.

2.45
12.05   15.02
       12.45   12.5

2 Compare each pair of numbers using the symbols < and >.
  a −5 and 7   b −7 and −11   c −10 and 10

3 The temperature outside is −6°C.
  a The temperature inside is 17.5°C. How much warmer is it inside?
  b The temperature outside falls another 4°. What is the temperature now?

B Fractions

1 Which of these fractions are equivalent?

$\frac{2}{5}$ $\frac{6}{8}$ $\frac{1}{3}$ 0.75   0.4 $\frac{3}{9}$

2 a Write these improper fractions as mixed numbers.

$\frac{8}{5}$ $\frac{10}{8}$ $\frac{7}{3}$ $\frac{11}{4}$ $\frac{13}{10}$ $\frac{12}{9}$

  b Copy this number line. Then order the mixed numbers and place them on it.

```
├────────┬────────┬────────┤
0        1        2        3
```

  c What proportion of the mixed numbers are greater than two?

3 Order these fractions and decimals from smallest to largest.

  a $\frac{3}{10}$ 0.03 $\frac{1}{2}$ 0.4 $\frac{7}{100}$

  b $\frac{50}{100}$ 0.05 $\frac{5}{10}$ 0.25 $\frac{3}{4}$

4 Write these percentages.
  a 50% of $420   b 25% of 420g   c 10% of 150g   d 20% of $150

5 In a pack of mixed drinks, there are two orange drinks for every three lemon drinks.
  a How many orange drinks are there in five packs?
  b How many lemon drinks are there in ten packs?

C Addition and subtraction

1 Use rounding and adjusting to complete these calculations.
  a 234 + 48 =   b 234 − 48 =   c 2345 + 199 =   d 2345 − 295 =

2 Find the difference between these pairs of numbers.
  a 803 and 699   b 142 and 129   c 905 and 788   d 1000 and 695

3 Complete these calculations.
  a 3645 + 1867 =   b 3645 − 1867 =   c 458 + 325 + 167 =
  d 34.83 + 23.18 =   e 39.83 − 6.47 =   f 87 + 655 + 45 + 329 =

Unit 12 Measures and problem solving

12a The metric system

Explore

Will an equal number of millilitres of milk and water have the same mass?

Converting, comparing and ordering measurements

Learn

When you compare measurements, it is important that you use what you know about converting between different units.

Here is a table showing the height of five different sunflowers.

Sunflower	A	B	C	D	E
Height	1.4 m	990 mm	$1\frac{1}{4}$ m	148 cm	1.05 m

Remember that 100 cm is equivalent to 1 m.

Which sunflower is closest to 1 m tall?

Key words

millimetre
centimetre
metre
kilometre
gram
kilogram
millilitre
litre

1 a What is the height of sunflowers A, C and E in centimetres (cm)?

   b What is the height of sunflowers B and D in metres (m)?

   c What is the height of each sunflower rounded to the nearest 0.1 m?

2 The tape measure shows the height of another sunflower, F.

   a What is the height of sunflower F?

   b How much taller is sunflower F than sunflower B?

   c Put the six sunflowers in order from shortest to tallest using metres (m).

Reading different scales

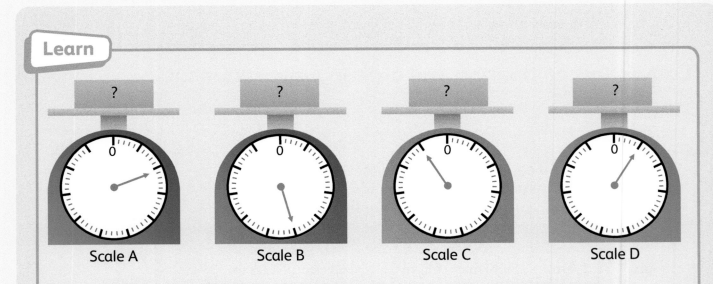

Scale A   Scale B   Scale C   Scale D

Is it possible for each of these weighing scales to show a mass with the same value?

Practise

1 Answer these questions.

   a When the mass on each scale is 1 kg, what are the larger intervals worth on Scale A?

   b When the mass on each scale is 50 g, what are the larger intervals worth on Scale B?

2 If the large intervals on Scale C go up in steps of 50 g, what is the value of the last interval? Remember that the mass on each scale is the same.

3 The mass on this scale is 2.5 kg.

What is the mass of objects A and B on the same weighing scale?

a

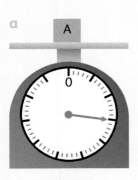

b

Think like a mathematician

You could start by thinking about intervals of 100 g to help you make decisions about possible scales.

Try this

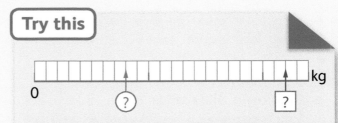

The value of the circle is greater than 1 kg but less than 5 kg.

   a Find at least five different possible values for the circle.

      What are the intervals and the value of the square each time?

   b Explain why the value of the square cannot be 2.2 kg.

12b Length, area and perimeter

Explore

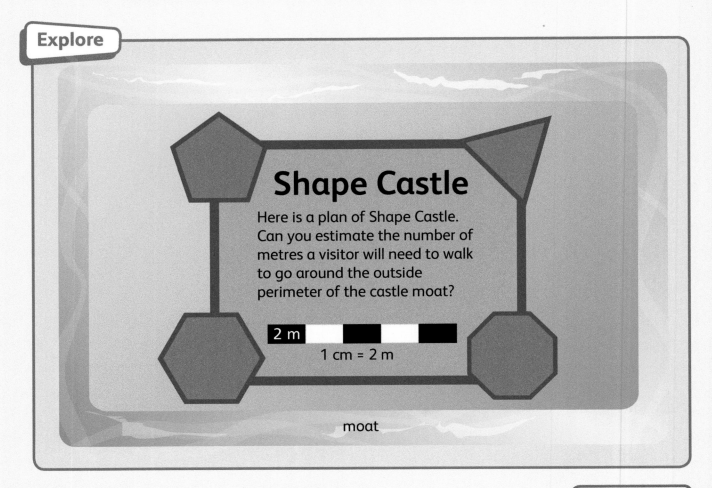

Shape Castle

Here is a plan of Shape Castle. Can you estimate the number of metres a visitor will need to walk to go around the outside perimeter of the castle moat?

2 m

1 cm = 2 m

moat

Calculating areas and perimeters

Learn

The plan shows towers in each corner of the castle.

I think that shapes with more sides will have longer perimeters. Am I right?

Key words

area
perimeter
polygon
regular
formula
metres
squared

Practise

1 Write the perimeter of each polygon shape:

a in metres

b in centimetres

c in millimetres.

2 Estimate the area of the base of each tower.
Each square on the grid has an area of 1 m².

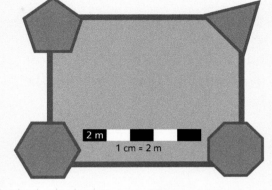

2 m
1 cm = 2 m

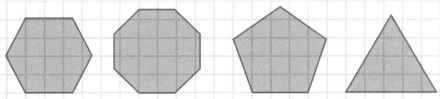

Try this

Each tower of the castle has a rectangular flag of a different size and colour.

	Red	Blue	Green	Yellow
Longer side			99 cm	80 cm
Shorter side	45 cm			

Use the clues to find the dimensions and area of each flag.

- The longer side on the blue flag is double the shorter side on the red flag.
- The shorter side on the green flag is 25 cm longer than the shorter side on the yellow flag.
- The area of the yellow flag is 480 cm².
- The longer side on the green flag is 1 cm shorter than the longer side on the green flag.
- The blue flag and the red flag have the same area.

Think like a mathematician

Read all the clues first to find the best starting point.

 12c Time

Explore

Shape Castle is a very popular tourist attraction.

Here is part of a train timetable to help visitors plan their journey to the castle.

Liddon	--	11:54	--	12:24	--	12:54
Berryton	--	12:17	--	12:47	--	13:17
Regents River	--	12:40	--	13:10	--	13:40
Biston	12:39	12:54	13:09	13:24	13:39	13:54
Yellow Park	12:51	13:06	13:21	13:36	13:51	14:06
Bankstown	13:15	13:30	13:45	14:00	14:15	14:30
Shape Castle	13:38	13:53	14:08	14:23	14:38	14:53

Does the journey from Yellow Park to Shape Castle always take 47 minutes?

Key words

second
minute
hour
day
week
month
fortnight
analogue clock
digital clock
duration
interval
calendar
timetable

Solving problems about time

Learn

Partitioning can help us check the time on 24-hour clocks.

The 13 hours in the time 13:24 can be partitioned into 12 hours and 1 hour.

Why do you think it is not partitioned into 10 hours and 3 hours?

The 12 hours are the hours in the morning from midnight to midday.

The 1 hour shows how many hours in the afternoon have passed.

So 13:24 is the same as 1:24 p.m.

> A visitor takes the 13:24 train from Biston. What time is this using the 12-hour digital clock?

 p.m.

1 What are each of these times using the 12-hour clock?

Remember to use a.m. (morning) and p.m. (afternoon).

a 08:47   b 20:47   c 11:05

d 23:05   e 14:00   f 00:00

2 Use the timetable on page 142 to calculate the duration of each journey.

a Take the 13:17 train from Berryton to Bankstown.

b Take the 12:24 train from Liddon to Shape Castle.

c Take the 12:40 train from Regents River to Shape Castle.

d Take the 12:54 train from Biston to Yellow Park.

3 It is five-to-one in the afternoon.

How many minutes will a passenger have to wait for the next train from:

a Berryton

b Regents River

c Biston

d Bankstown?

Solving problems using calendars

March						2014
Sun	Mon	Tues	Wed	Thu	Fri	Sat
						1
2	3	4	5	6	7	8
9	10	11	12	13	14	15
16	17	18	19	20	21	22
23	24	25	26	27	28	29
30	31					

February						2014
Sun	Mon	Tues	Wed	Thu	Fri	Sat
						1
2	3	4	5	6	7	8
9	10	11	12	13		15
16	17	18	19	20	21	22
23	24	25	26	27	28	

Shape Castle was first opened to the public on 10 March 2014. How long ago was that?

Practise

1 Solve these problems

   a A television show was filmed at Shape Castle a fortnight before it opened.

      What date was this?

   b The ten-thousandth visitor to Shape Castle visited on 27 July 2014.

      If the opening day on 10 March is Day 1, what day is 27 July?

   c Afia visited Shape Castle in the sixth week after opening day.

      What are the possible dates on which she could have visited the castle?

2 Orlando visited the castle on 14 June 2014. He thinks it was a Sunday.

   Is Orlando correct?

3 Orlando visited the castle on 14 June 2014.

   Afia visited the castle 60 days before Orlando.

   What day was this?

Think like a mathematician

Remember to think about the number of weeks in a year. Do not forget that there is an extra day every four years when we have a leap year, so be careful of dates in leap years.

Try this

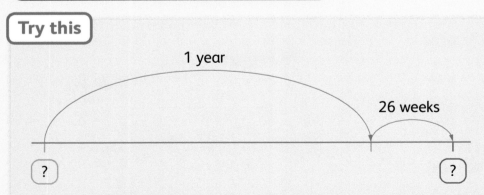

How can you prove that the two missing dates here are not 15 February 2014 and 15 July 2015?

What could the dates be? Try to find at least five solutions.

Self-check

A The metric system

1. 3 265 g   3.4 kg   3.25 kg   3 500 g
   a Order these masses from lightest to heaviest.
   b Now round the masses to the nearest kilogram (kg).

2. Convert these measurements into the units shown.
   a 2 345 g to kilograms (kg)
   b 2.75 ℓ to millilitres (ml)
   c 12.5 m to centimetres (cm)
   d 250 mm to centimetres (cm)

3. What are the values of measurements A, B and C on this container?

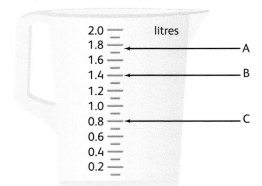

B Length, area and perimeter

1. Measure these two lines.

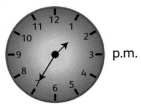

   a What is the approximate difference between the lengths of these lines?
   b Orlando draws a 35 cm line.
      Afia draws a regular pentagon with a perimeter of the same length. What is the length of each side of the pentagon?

2. What is the approximate total area of the coloured parts of this flag?

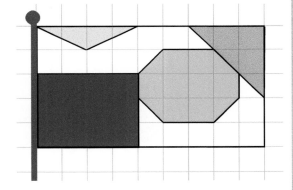

C Time

1. Look at the time shown on the clock.

   p.m.

   How long must the visitors wait to go on these different tours at Shape Castle?

Garden Tour	Art Tour	Special Tour	History Tour
13:45	14:15	14:30	15:00

2. a How many weeks are equal to 84 days?
   b How many months are there in $2\frac{1}{2}$ years?

3. The date is 19 October.
   a What was the date exactly 3 weeks ago?
   b How many days is it until 20 November?

13a Number patterns

Here is a pattern of beads.

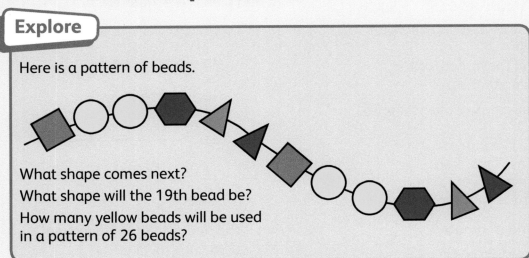

What shape comes next?

What shape will the 19th bead be?

How many yellow beads will be used in a pattern of 26 beads?

Key words ⟳

sequence

rule

term

position

next

previous

multiple

Exploring patterns and sequences

The position of each bead in the pattern can be given a number. The first square bead is number one, and the first circular bead is number two.

The beads in the odd number positions in this pattern will never be blue.

Do you agree?

How can you work this out?

1 The start of the sequence for the position of the blue triangle beads is 6, 12, 18 …

  a Write the first five terms in the sequence for the positions of:

    ● red square beads

    ● blue hexagon beads

    ● green triangle beads.

  b What is the rule each time?

2 The numbers show the position of some beads in the sequence.

  a One bead is incorrectly numbered each time. Which one is it?

| 25 | 37 | 56 | 61 | 34 | 48 | 64 | 70 |

  b What is the correct shape and colour for the wrong bead numbers you found?

The cost of each yellow round bead is 12 cents.
The cost of each red square bead is 20 cents.

How much more will be spent on yellow round beads than
red square beads in a pattern with a total of 100 beads?

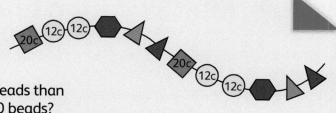

Finding and using rules for sequences

Learn

Look at this sequence of numbers: 8, _____, 14, _____, 20, _____

Working out the size of the equal steps to find the rule for this pattern is not quite as easy,
because some numbers are missing.

You can still find the difference between a pair of numbers to help you. The difference between
8 and 14 is 6. The difference between 14 and 20 is also 6, but the difference has to be split into
two equal steps each time.

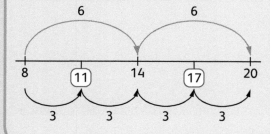

Practise

1 Find the rule and the missing terms for each
of these sequences.

a 3, ____, 11, ____, 19, ____

b 23, ____, 13, ____, 3, ____

c ____, 15, ____, 29, ____

d 3, ____, 6, ____, 9 , ____, ____

e 75 , ____, 25, ____, ____, −50

2 The rule for a sequence is subtract 50.

The first term is 1 000.

Why do I know
that the 12th term
cannot be a multiple
of 100 without
working it out?

13b **Multiplication and division**

Explore

The *Harmony of the Seas* made her maiden voyage in May 2016.
At the time, she was the largest cruise ship in the world.
It took workers 33 months to build the ship. Approximately, how many days is that?

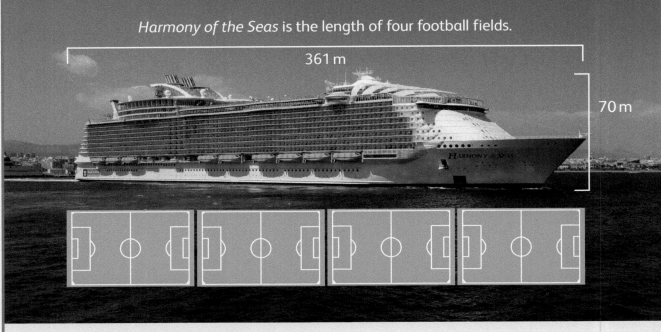

Harmony of the Seas is the length of four football fields.

361 m

70 m

What is the length of one football field?

Using multiples of 10 and 100

Learn

You can use multiplication facts and place value to help multiply multiples of 10 and 100.

60 × 9 is 10 times larger than 6 × 9.

You can also show this using factors of 60 as 6 × 10 × 9 or 6 × 9 × 10.

600 × 9 is 100 times larger than 6 × 9.

How can you rewrite this calculation using factors?

Key words

scale
product
divisible
remainder
inverse
square
multiple
factor
round
adjust

Practise

1 a Rewrite and solve each of these calculations using factors. The first one has been done
      for you. Work down the columns

30 × 5 =	3 × 10 × 5 = 3 × 5 × 10	40 × 4 =	40 × 8 =
300 × 5 =		400 × 4 =	400 × 8 =
60 × 5 =		80 × 4 =	80 × 8 =
600 × 5 =		800 × 4 =	800 × 8 =

   b What do you notice about the products of the calculations in the middle and last column?
      Can you quickly work out the answer to 40 × 16?

2 a How many spaces are
      available at each car park?

   b Car park F has 720 spaces.
      Look at the Key. Then work
      out how many car symbols
      will be needed to show this
      on the pictogram.

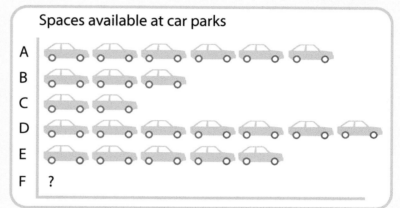

Spaces available at car parks

A, B, C, D, E, F ?

KEY

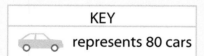 represents 80 cars

Try this

Follow the path of these calculations to find the value of
the question mark each time.

70	× 4	÷ 7	× 6	÷ 3	× 5	÷ 4	= ?

300	× 8	÷ 4	× 6	÷ 9	× 2	÷ ?	= 200

Think like a mathematician

Note down the answers you get for each step
along the path to help you keep track.

149

Multiplying by a near multiple of 10

Learn

The product of 23 × 19 is 2 less than the product of 23 × 21.

Do you agree?

Why do you think Orlando thinks this?

What can you draw to prove that he is wrong?

You can multiply by 19 or 21 by multiplying by 20 and adjusting.

23 × 19 is one group of 23 less than 23 × 20.

23 × 21 is one group of 23 more than 23 × 20.

Practise

1 Calculate the following. Work down the columns.

a 26 × 20 =

26 × 19 =

26 × 21 =

b 37 × 20 =

37 × 19 =

37 × 21 =

c 54 × 20 =

54 × 19 =

54 × 21 =

2 Afia's aunt is using patterned tiles to make a design. Each tile has a pattern made up of circles and squares. Complete the table to show the number of circles and squares each time.

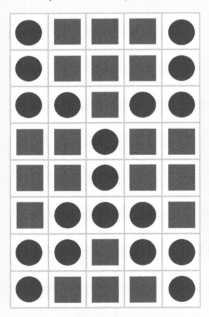

Copy and complete the table.

	1 tile	14 tiles	25 tiles	38 tiles	64 tiles
Number of circles	19				
Number of squares	21				
Total number of shapes	40				

Multiplying by 25

Learn

Afia has saved 32 of these coins in her money box.

What method can you use to find out how much money she has in total?

Why is multiplying by 25 the same as multiplying by 100 and dividing by 4?

Can you divide by 4 first and then multiply by 100?

Practise

1 Find the total value of each number of 25 cent coins.

   a 18 coins   b 45 coins

   c 53 coins   d 68 coins

   e How many 25 cent coins make a total of 475 cents?

2 The area of a small square is 25 cm².

25 cm²

What is the total area of the purple shape?

Think like a mathematician

Remember to decide whether is is easier to multiply by 100 first and then divide by 4 or divide by 4 first and then multiply by 100.

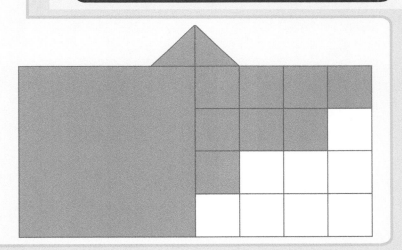

Using factors to multiply

Learn

What multiplication calculations are represented here? How do you know?
What is the same and what is different about them?

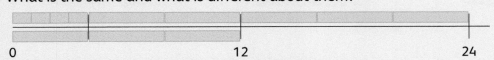

0   12   24

The product of 4 × 6 is double the product of 4 × 3.
You can rewrite 4 × 6 as 4 × 3 × 2 using factors.

In the same way, the product of 16 × 7 is double the product of 8 × 7.
You can rewrite 16 × 7 as 2 × 8 × 7 or 8 × 7 × 2.

Practise

1   Rewrite each of these calculations using factors and then solve them. Work down the columns. The first one has been done for you.

15 × 6 = 3 × 5 × 6 = 90   9 × 14 =   8 × 14 =

16 × 6 =   9 × 16 =   16 × 8 =

19 × 6 =   9 × 18 =   8 × 19 =

23 × 6 =   9 × 24 =   22 × 8 =

2   Apples, lemons and limes are stacked in boxes.

What is the total number of fruit in each stack of boxes?

	18 lemons	
	18 lemons	40 limes
24 apples	18 lemons	40 limes
24 apples	18 lemons	40 limes
24 apples	18 lemons	40 limes
24 apples	18 lemons	40 limes
24 apples	18 lemons	40 limes
24 apples	18 lemons	40 limes
a	b	c

3   Here are some function machines.

Write the missing function and outputs.

a

× 4 × 2

b

× ___ × 2

c

× 4 × 2

Try this

Orlando's uncle is twice the age of his cousin.

His cousin is three times the age of his sister.

His sister is five times older than his pet cat.

a   How many times older is Orlando's uncle than his pet cat?

b   How many times older is Orlando's uncle than his sister?

c   How many times older is his cousin than his pet cat?

Find two sets of possible ages for this group of people and the pet cat.

Doubling and halving

Learn

Here is a pasta recipe for four people:

Write the recipe for eight people.
And now write it for two people.

400 g dried pasta
4 large eggs
90 g soft cheese
I lemon
120 g fresh or frozen peas
150 g spinach

Practise

1 Halve each of these numbers.

Work down the columns.

a	64	b	56	c	85
	640		560		850
	6 400		5 600		8 500
	6.4		5.6		8.5

2 The nutrition in the pasta meal for **one** person is shown here.

Calories	Fat	Saturates	Protein	Carbs	Sugar	Salt	Fibre
463	9.4 g	2.5 g	22.4 g	77.5 g	4.5 g	0.3 g	4.9 g

What are the nutritional values for the recipe for **two** people?

3 Here is part of another nutrition label.

	100 g provides	50 g ($\frac{1}{4}$ of a pot) provides
Fat	18.8 g	
of which: saturates	2.4 g	
Carbohydrates	13.6 g	
of which: sugars	0.3 g	
Protein	9.5 g	
Salt	1.2 g	

a Calculate the missing values for a 50 g serving.

b What is the total mass of the whole pot?

c How many grams of fat are in the whole pot?

Turning remainders into fractions

Learn

Here are two representations for the calculation 85 ÷ 4 where 4 is the divisor.

There is a remainder of one because another group of four 'ones' cannot be made.

The remainder of one can also be divided by four but the answer will result in a fraction.

This can be represented in two ways. One way is sharing one whole into four equal parts. The other way is grouping to show one out of a group of the divisor four.

$1 \div 4 = \frac{1}{4}$

So $85 \div 4 = 21\frac{1}{4}$

You can check the answer to a division using multiplication.

21 × 4 = 84 and add the remainder 1 to give 85.

Practise

1 The pictures below show the remainders after some division calculations. The remainder in each whole group is shaded orange. Write the remainder each time and turn it into a fraction.

a  b   c  d

2 Complete these calculations. Turn any remainders into fractions.
Check each calculation using multiplication.

a 65 ÷ 3 = b 66 ÷ 4 = c 66 ÷ 5 = d 68 ÷ 7 = e 69 ÷ 8 =

3 Solve these word problems. Will you need to round the remainder or turn it into a fraction?

a Balls come in boxes of 25. Afia puts them in bags of four.
How many bags of four balls are there?

b A 48 m length of rope is cut into five equal pieces. What is the length of each piece?

c 78 ml of water is divided equally between eight containers.
How many millilitres of water are in each container?

d There are six eggs in a box. How many boxes are needed for 94 eggs?

e There are 48 strawberries in a bag. Five children eat an equal number of the strawberries.
How many strawberries are left in the bag?

Try this

The remainder after a division calculation is turned into a fraction $\frac{2}{5}$. $\boxed{} \div \boxed{} = \boxed{} \frac{2}{5}$

Find at least five ways to make this true.

Look for any patterns in your solutions and write a rule that can be used to find other possible solutions.

Think like a mathematician

Find a useful starting point to explore the problem. What is the lowest value to be divided that would result in the remainder $\frac{2}{5}$. Think about sketching the remainder in the same way that is used in Practise question 1 on page 154.

Using brackets

Learn

You have used partitioning and factorising in this unit to help solve multiplication problems.

You use brackets in calculations to organise the parts of the calculation and to show what part needs to be done first.

Look at the way brackets are used here to organise each part of the calculation.

$120 \times 2 = (100 \times 2) + (20 \times 2)$

Brackets have the highest priority. Do the operation inside them **before** you do the multiplication or division. Always do addition or subtraction last, unless they are inside a bracket.

You can also use brackets for the calculation 6×14. What is the same and what is different each time? Which is easier?

$6 \times 14 = 6 \times (7 \times 2)$ $6 \times 14 = (6 \times 7) \times 2$

Practise

1 Double each of these numbers by partitioning. Use brackets to organise each part of the calculation.

a 45   b 145   c 105   d 4.5   e 6.45.

2 Solve the calculations. Remember to do the parts in brackets first.

a $25 \times (5 + 5) =$
b $(25 \times 5) + 5 =$
c $25 \times (4 \times 5) =$
d $(25 \times 4) \times 5 =$
e $(100 - 50) \div 2 =$
f $100 - (50 \div 2) =$

3 Use brackets to keep track of the calculations.

a Afia has 150 cents. She buys three pencils at 25 cents each. How much money does she have left?

b Orlando bakes 48 cookies. He puts 28 cookies in a box and 20 cookies in a bag. Half of the cookies in the box are eaten.

How many cookies are left altogether?

Try this

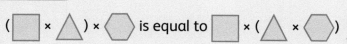 $(\boxed{} \times \triangle) \times \hexagon$ is equal to $\boxed{} \times (\triangle \times \hexagon)$ Is this statement always, sometimes or never true? Put in your own numbers to investigate.

Self-check

A Number patterns

1 The **second** term in a sequence is 40. The rule is **add** 12.
Write the **first five terms** in the sequence.

2 The rule of a sequence is **subtract** ten.
The first term is 123. Predict the 8th term.

3 Find the rule for this sequence and write the next **five** terms.
10.1, 12.6, 15.1, 17.6

B Multiplication and division

1 Use factors to help you multiply.
a $5 \times 18 =$ b $24 \times 9 =$ c $36 \times 4 =$

2 Change the remainder each time into a fraction.
a $124 \div 5 =$ b $248 \div 6 =$ c $465 \div 10 =$

3 If we divide \$456 equally between two people, how much will each person get?
What is the inverse calculation you can use to check your answer?

4 Which calculation has the largest answer?
a $8 \times 5 \times 3 =$ b $8 \times (5 + 3) =$
c $8 \times (5 \times 3) =$ d $(8 \times 5) + 3 =$

Unit 14   Geometry and problem solving

14a Classifying 2-D shapes

Explore

Are all these flags the same type of triangle? What do I need to know to help me check?

Key words
scalene
isosceles
equilateral
right-angled
reflective symmetry
rotational symmetry

Solving problems about triangles

Learn

Afia and Orlando want to make their own string of different triangular flags.

They want to use four **equal** sized equilateral triangles, three isosceles triangles and two scalene triangles.

What is the same and what is different about each of these types of triangles?

Practise

1 The children have only two pieces of cloth to make all the flags, so they need to use them carefully.

How can they cut the pieces of cloth to make all the flags they need?

Reflective and rotational symmetry

Learn

Afia and Orlando decide to make flags using different shapes.

Here are some of the shapes they will use:

Afia's string of flags can only have shapes with reflective and rotational symmetry.

Orlando's string of flags can have shapes with only reflective symmetry.

Which of these shapes can each child use?

Practise

1 a Find five other shapes that Afia can use for her string of flags.

b Find five other shapes that Orlando can use for his string of flags.

2 Draw three other shapes that neither child can use.

14b **3-D and 2-D shapes**

Explore

I found pairs of parallel lines and perpendicular lines on the edges of the faces of some 3-D shapes.

Which 3-D shapes could they be?
Which ones could they not be?

Key words

symmetry

net

open

closed

parallel

perpendicular

angles

vertex

Symmetrical patterns

Learn

A pattern is symmetrical when it has one or more lines of symmetry.
When we place a mirror on the line of symmetry, the reflected image completes the pattern exactly.

Which of these patterns are symmetrical? Where is the line of symmetry?

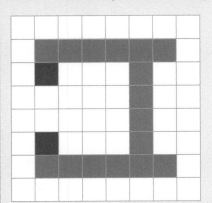 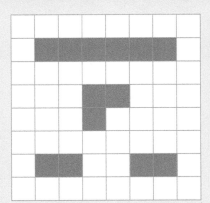 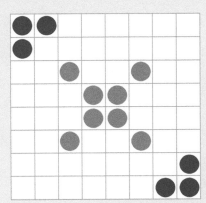

Practise

1 Use squared paper or a peg board to make the second pattern on page 159.

 a Add one more square or peg to make the pattern symmetrical.

 How many lines of symmetry does the pattern have?

 b Add **two** more squares or pegs so that the pattern now has **two** lines of symmetry.

 c Add another **four** squares or pegs so that the pattern still has **two** lines of symmetry.

2 Use squared paper or a peg board to make a pattern each time that has:

 a no lines of symmetry

 b one line of symmetry

 c two lines of symmetry

 d four lines of symmetry.

Think like a mathematician

Remember that you can use a mirror to check your patterns, and also think about lines of symmetry that are in a diagonal position.

More about nets

Learn

Remember, a net is a two-dimensional pattern of polygons that can be folded to form a three-dimensional shape.

You can use these polygons to make the nets of some 3-D shapes.

Which polygons can you use to make the net of a cuboid?

How many of each will you need?

Practise

1 Which of the polygons from page 160 can you use now to make nets for these 3-D shapes?

Remember to say how many of each polygon is needed.

a Cube

b Triangular prism

c Hexagonal prism.

2 We can use the same polygons to make nets for other 3-D shapes.

a Which two shapes are they?

b Can you arrange the polygons in a different way and still make the nets for these 3-D shapes?

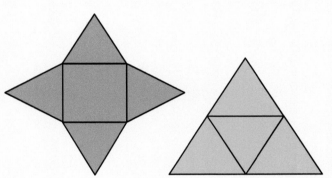

Angles

Learn

Angles show the amount of turn between two lines that form a vertex. Angles are measured in degrees. One whole turn is 360° or four right angles.

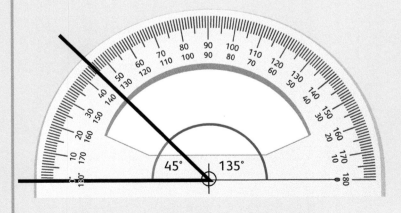

We use a protractor to measure angles. This protractor has a scale from 0° to 180° labelled at every 10° but with marks at every 1°.

The two lines that meet at the bottom of the protractor make a straight line. This angle is 180° and is made up of two right angles.

The 45° angle shown here is called an acute angle because it is less than 90°. The 135° angle that completes the straight line is called an obtuse angle. It is greater than 90° but less than 180°.

Practise

1 a What is the size and name of each angle? Remember to make an estimate first.

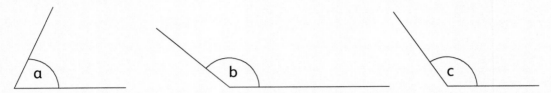

b How many degrees larger would each of these angles need to be to make a straight line?

2 a Estimate, measure and name these angles.

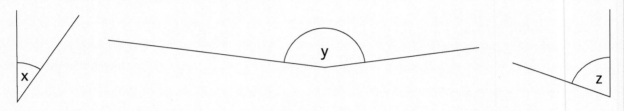

b How many degrees smaller than a full turn is each angle?

3 Here are the first three terms in a sequence of angles.

a What is the size of the next two angles in the sequence? What is the rule?

b Draw the next two angles carefully.

Try this

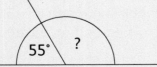

How can you work out the size of this angle without measuring it?

Think like a mathematician

Use what you know about right angles to help make an estimate.

14c Working with coordinates

Explore

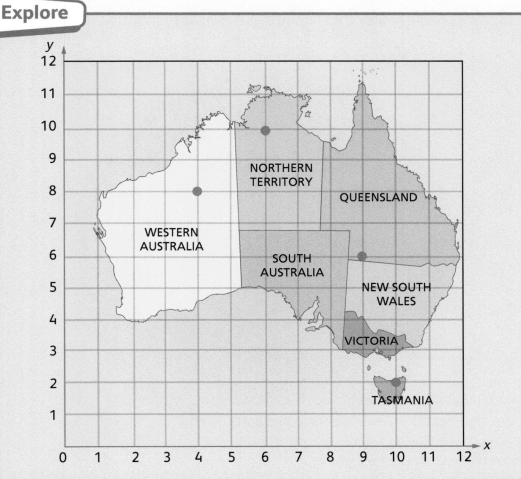

What are the coordinates of the four locations shown on this map of Australia?

In which state can the coordinates (4, 8) be found?

What other coordinates can you give for other locations on this map?

Solving problems about coordinates

Learn

Remember that a coordinate gives a point's reference on each axis and is written as a pair inside brackets (x, y).

What is the same and what is different about this set of coordinates?

(4, 3), (4, 5), (4, 7) and (4, 9)

What pattern will they make when plotted on a coordinate grid? How do you know?

Practise

1 Afia and Orlando use a coordinate grid for their nature trail. Answer the questions about coordinates.

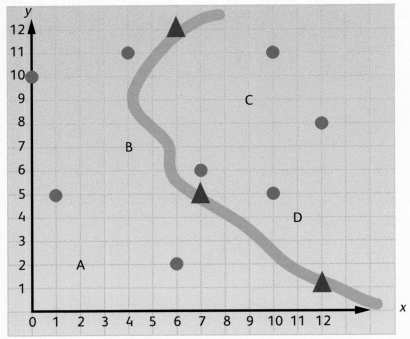

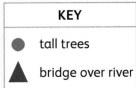

KEY	
●	tall trees
▲	bridge over river

a What are the coordinates of the three tall trees that are closest to location D?

b Where can the children cross the river? Give the coordinates.

c The letters A, B, C and D show good places to take photographs.
   What letter is shown at coordinate (4, 7)?

2 Afia, Orlando and their friend each visit three tall trees. No trees are left out.

> i   The trees that Afia visits give the vertices of an isosceles triangle on the map.
> ii   The trees that Orlando visits makes a different isosceles triangle.
> iii Their friend's trees make a scalene triangle on the map.

a Give the coordinates of the trees visited by their friend.

b Afia and Orlando both visit the same tall tree. What are the coordinates?

Remember to use what you know about the properties of different triangles to help you.

Think like a mathematician

When we use maps, we turn them around to look at them in different ways. This is called orientating the map.

⏻ 14d Transformations

Explore

Try reflecting the triangle in different mirror lines. Can you predict the position of the reflected shape each time?

Key words ⏻
transformation
reflection
mirror line
translation

Using reflections and translations

Learn

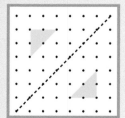 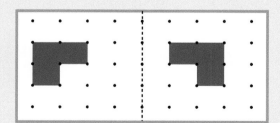 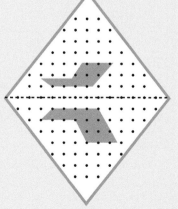

A new exhibition is taking place in an art gallery.

All the paintings show polygons reflected in different mirror lines.

Which of these paintings cannot go in the exhibition? Why?

Practise

1 Here are two more pictures that cannot go in the exhibition.

Explain what is wrong with each one and draw the correct version.

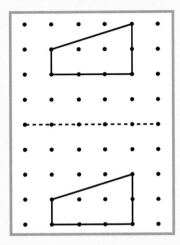

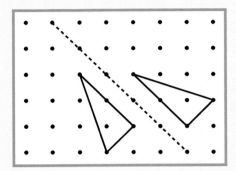

2 Sketch one reflection picture of your own that can go in the exhibition and one reflection picture that cannot go in the exhibition.

Challenge a friend to spot the correct one and to explain what is wrong with the other picture.

3 Here are some other paintings in the exhibition. These paintings are moved each week.

The grids show the positions of the paintings in Week 1 and Week 2.

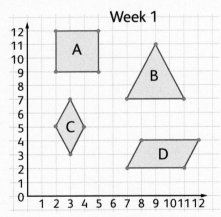

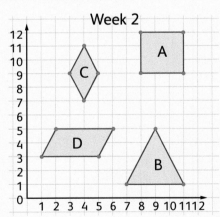

a Describe the translation of each painting from Week 1 to Week 2.

b On Week 3, painting A is translated 3 squares left and 5 squares down from its position in Week 2. What are the coordinates of each vertex of the painting?

Self-check

A Classifying 2-D shapes

1 Here are five different triangles.

 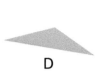

A   B   C   D   E

a Name each triangle.
b Which triangles have reflective and rotational symmetry?
c Which triangles have only reflective symmetry?
d Which triangles do not have either reflective or rotational symmetry?

B 3-D and 2-D shapes

1 a How many lines of symmetry does this pattern have?
b How many pairs of parallel lines can you find that make up the sides of the coloured shapes?
c How many pairs of perpendicular lines can you find that make up the sides of the coloured shapes?
d Estimate, measure and name the angles on one of the trapezia.

2 Sketch the nets for a triangular prism and a cuboid.

C Working with coordinates

1 Write the coordinates of letters A, C and D on the map of the nature trail on page 164.

2 Orlando takes another photograph at location (5, 9) on the map.
He then crosses the nearest bridge.

What are the coordinates of this bridge?

D Transformations

1 What are the coordinates of the shapes after the reflection in the mirror line?

2 Translate the original square 1 square left and 2 squares down.
What are its new coordinates?

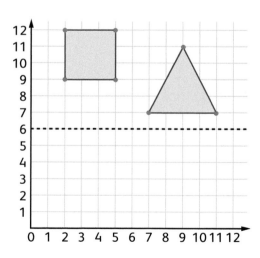

Unit 15   Problem solving and review

15a Problem solving

Explore

All the problems in this unit are about a camping trip.

This is a tent for two adults. What would be a good estimate for the area of ground it covers?

On the way

1 Afia and her aunt are packing for a camping trip. They pack exactly 5 kg of food.

What could they pack?

| $\frac{1}{2}$ kg | 0.4 kg | 420 g | 540 g | 700 g | 750 g | 0.25 kg |

2 The diagram shows the journey by car from Afia's aunt's house to the campsite.

The total length of the journey is 150 km.

a How far is it from Afia's aunt's house to the fueling station in kilometres (km)?

b Now write this distance in metres (m).

c The car uses 3.75 litres of fuel for every 50 km of the journey.
How many litres of fuel will be used for the total journey?

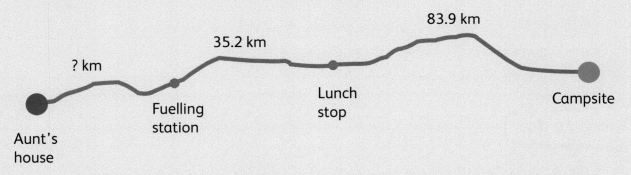

3 Afia and her aunt stop for 45 minutes for lunch and spend five minutes at the fuelling station.
It takes them approximately 12 minutes to drive 10 km.

a Approximately how long does the journey take from Afia's aunt's house to the campsite?

b Afia and her aunt set off at 09:55.

What time did they arrive at the campsite?

Give the time using the 24-hour clock notation.

At the campsite

1 The pictogram shows the number of each type of tent at the campsite.

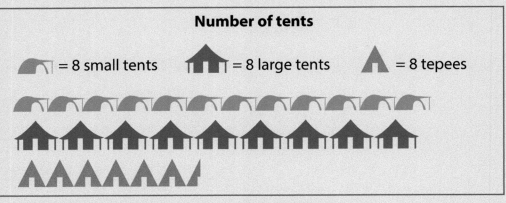

Number of tents

= 8 small tents   = 8 large tents   = 8 tepees

a How many more small tents are there than tepees?

b How many tents are there in total?

c Tepee tents can sleep up to six people.
What is the greatest number of people that can sleep in the tepees?

d A school party of 90 children arrives at the campsite.
A large tent sleeps seven people.
How many large tents are needed for 90 children?

2 A group of 100 people can fill large tents and tepees with nobody left over.

Is this statement always, sometimes or never true?

How will you prove your answer is correct?

Things to do

1 There are lots of activities to do on Saturday. Each activity lasts 40 minutes.

Afia would like to do all of the activities on that day. Plan her timetable for the day.

Be prepared to explain how you know that your plan for the day is possible.

Activity	Times			
	Session 1	Session 2	Session 3	Session 4
Swimming	13:40	14:40	15:40	16:40
Treasure hunt	14:15	15:05	16:10	16:50
Rowing races	13:50	14:50	15:50	16:55
Nature trail	14:30	15:25	16:15	17:10
Camp fire songs	14:05	14:55	15:55	17:00

2 All 90 children in the school group take part in the activities during Session 1 and Session 2.

Use the information in the table to find out how many children did each of the activities during the sessions.

	Session 1	Session 2
Swimming	10 % of group	$\frac{3}{10}$ of group
Treasure hunt	0	40 % of group
Rowing races	$\frac{1}{3}$ of group	$\frac{1}{5}$ of group
Nature trail	$\frac{2}{5}$ of group	0
Camp fire songs	$\frac{1}{6}$ of group	$\frac{1}{10}$ of group
Total children:	90	90

3 During the treasure hunt, the children find different shapes that they must use to complete a mystery picture.

a Use the clues to work out the position of each of the six shapes.

Shape 1 has rotational symmetry but no parallel lines.

Shape 2 has no rotational symmetry but has one pair of parallel lines.

Shape 3 has two pairs of parallel and perpendicular lines.

Shape 4 has reflective symmetry and more than two pairs of parallel lines.

Shape 5 has no rotational symmetry and no perpendicular lines.

Shape 6 has four lines of reflective symmetry.

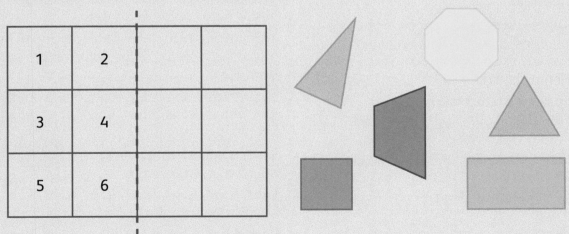

b The mystery picture is completed by reflecting the pattern of shapes in the vertical mirror line. Sketch the complete mystery pattern on paper.

Mathematical dictionary

2-D 2-dimensional; a flat shape with sides and angles

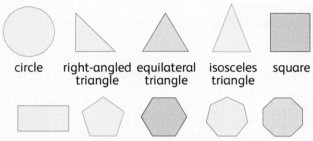

circle | right-angled triangle | equilateral triangle | isosceles triangle | square

rectangle | pentagon | hexagon | heptagon | octagon

3-D 3-dimensional; a solid shape with faces, edges and vertices

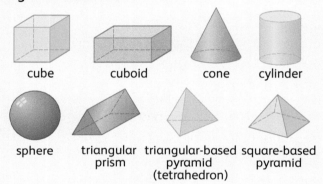

cube | cuboid | cone | cylinder

sphere | triangular prism | triangular-based pyramid (tetrahedron) | square-based pyramid

A

addition a calculation in which you add one thing to another

adjust when you do calculations in your head, you often round off numbers to make the calculation easier and then you have to adjust the answer at the end

analogue clock a clock that displays the time by using moving hands and hours marked from 1 to 12 on a clock face

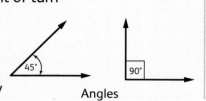

Analogue clock

angles The amount of turn between two straight lines that join each other; you measure the angle in degrees by

Angles

working out the amount that you would need to turn one line to sit exactly on top of the other line

area the amount of space that a flat surface or a shape covers

C

calendar a set of pages or tables that show the days, weeks and months of a year

capacity the amount of space that a container has to hold things

Celsius a temperature scale on which water freezes at 0° and boils at 100°

centimetres a unit for measuring the length of something; 100 centimetres = 1 metre.

centimetre squared a unit for measuring area; 1 cm² = a square measuring one centimetre on each side

Centimetre squared

certain definite

check make sure, do the calculation again

collect and organise we gather (collect) information (data) in order to find answers to questions; then we arrange (organise) it in such a way that other people can understand it easily, for example in a table

continuous data information that can have any value within a range, for example time or distance

coordinates show the position of a point on a grid with an x-axis and a y-axis, for example (4,2)

cube a box-shaped object with six square faces that are all the same length

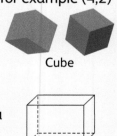

Cube

cuboid a box-shaped object with six faces of the same or different lengths, for example a rectangular prism and a cube are both cuboids

Cuboid

D

data information

decimal a number less than 1; decimals are shown by using a full stop, or comma, followed by tenths, hundredths, etc.; example: 0.1 means one tenth

decimal place the position of a digit to the right of a decimal point; example: 0.214 has three decimal places and 4 is in the third decimal place

denominator a number below the line in a fraction, also called the divisor

difference the answer you get when you subtract one number from another

digit one of the written signs we use to represent the numbers 0 to 9

digital clock a clock that displays the time using digits; these clocks do not have moving hands. It can display time using either a 12-hour or 24-hour system

Digital clock

discrete data data that can be counted in whole numbers or categories, for example the number of people, cars or animals

divide to find how many times a number is contained in another number

divisible when a number can be divided by another number without leaving a remainder

division separating something into parts

duration the length of time during which something continues

E

equally likely when events are equally likely, they have the same theoretical chance of happening

equilateral a shape with sides that are all the same length

equivalent the same value as

estimate to try to judge the value, size, amount, cost, speed, etc. of something without calculating it exactly

even number a number that is divisible by 2

even chance when there is an equal chance that something might happen or might not happen

F

factor a whole number that divides into another whole number exactly

first quadrant the space on a coordinate grid where both the x- and the y-values are positive

formula a series of numbers or letters that represents a rule in mathematics

fortnight two weeks

fraction a part of something or a part of a number

G

gram the basic unit for measuring weight in the metric system; 1000 grams = 1 kilogram

greater than more than

H

height how tall a person or object is

hour a unit used for measuring time; 1 hour = 60 minutes

hundred ten groups of ten

hundredth one part of something that has been divided equally into a hundred parts or is shrunk to be 100 times smaller

I

impossible cannot be done, cannot happen

improper fraction a fraction in which the numerator (the top number) is greater than or equal to the denominator (the bottom number), for example $\frac{3}{2}$

interval time or space between two events

inverse the opposite of an operation, for example subtraction is the inverse of addition

isosceles triangle a triangle that has two sides of equal length

Isosceles triangle

K

kilogram a unit for measuring weight;
1 kilogram = 1 000 grams

kilometre a unit for measuring distance;
1 kilometre = 1 000 metres

L

length the measurement of how long
something is from one point to another point

less than not as many as

likely probable; a good chance that something
may happen

M

mass a measure of how much matter
(material) is in an object; mass can be measured
in grams and kilograms

metre a unit for measuring length or distance

metre squared a unit for measuring area;
$1m^2$ = a square that measures one metre on
each side

millilitre a unit for measuring volume;
1000 millilitres = 1 litre

millimetre a unit for measuring length;
1 000 millimetres = 1 metre

minute a unit for measuring time; 60 min = 1 hr

mirror line the central line over which you flip a
shape when you create a mirror image

mixed number a number that consists of a
whole number and a fraction, for example $5\frac{3}{4}$

mode the value that appears most often in a
set of data

month a unit for measuring time, ranging
between 29 days and 31 days

multiple a number that contains a smaller
number an exact number of times; for example:
25 is a multiple of 5

multiplication a method of calculation that
involves scaling a number or quantity, for
example, doubling is scaling a number by two
and multiplying by 10 is making a number ten
times larger; it can also sometimes be described
as adding a number to itself a specific number
of times

multiply calculate the product of two numbers

N

nearest multiple of ten when you round off
a number to the nearest multiple of ten, you
take it up or down to its closest multiple of 10.
Example: 76 rounded off to its closest multiple
of 10 would be 80 and 74 rounded off to its
nearest multiple of 10 would be 70

nearest whole number when you round off
a fraction or a decimal to the nearest whole
number, you take the number up or down to
the closest whole number. Example: $2\frac{3}{4}$ (2.75
in decimals) rounded off to the closest whole
number is 3 and $4\frac{1}{4}$ (4.25 in decimals) rounded
off to the nearest whole number is 4

negative numbers numbers less than zero

net a net is a two-dimensional
pattern of flat shapes that can
be folded to form a three-
dimensional shape

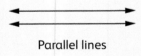

A net

numerator the number above
the line in a fraction; in the fraction $\frac{5}{6}$, 5 is the
numerator, also called the dividend

O

odd numbers whole numbers that are not
divisible by 2, for example 1, 3, 5, 7

P

parallel lines two lines that
are the same distance apart
along their whole length

Parallel lines

partition to break numbers
up into different parts, for example
you could partition the number 43512 into
40 000 + 3 000 + 500 + 10 + 2

percentage a number that is expressed as a
fraction of 100, for example if you score 70 %
for a test, you score 70 out of 100

perimeter perimeter is the
distance or path around a
two-dimensional (2-D) shape

perpendicular lines lines
that cut at 90 degrees

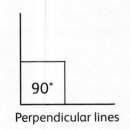

Perpendicular lines

place holder the digit 0, which holds other digits in the correct position so their value is known, for example in the number 356.024, zero holds the other digits in the correct position

place value the value that every digit has in a number, for example a one, a hundred or a thousand

polygon a flat shape with three or more straight sides

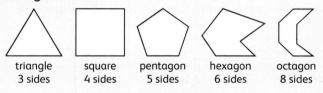

| triangle | square | pentagon | hexagon | octagon |
| 3 sides | 4 sides | 5 sides | 6 sides | 8 sides |

Examples of polygons

position the position of a digit is its place on the value grid or the exact position on a map or graph shown by coordinates. Example: the digit 1 is in the ten thousands position below and the digit 3 is in the hundreds position

Hundred thousands	Ten thousands	Thousands	Hundreds	Tens	Units
	1	7	3	3	5

The value grid

positive numbers numbers greater than zero

previous something that comes directly before the thing on which you are focusing now

probability how likely something is

problem a question to which you have to find the right answer by using mathematics or logical thought

product the number you get when you multiply two or more numbers

properties of shapes we describe 2-D shapes by referring to the number of sides, the length of the sides and the sizes of the angles

proportion a comparison between two numbers showing their relationship in terms of relative size, amount, position, etc.; proportions are shown as fractions

Q

quantity the amount of something that can be counted or measured

quotient the number you get when you divide one number by another

R

ratio a relationship between two amounts; the relationship is shown by using two numbers that tell you how many times bigger or smaller one amount is than the other

reflection when you reflect an object, you flip it to create a mirror image; each point of that mirror image is exactly the same distance away from the central line, called the mirror line, as the original object, but it is on the opposite side of the line

mirror line

shape   reflection

reflective symmetry when one half of a shape is a mirror image of the other

regular shape a polygon that has sides that are all equal and inside angles that are all equal

remainder the amount left over after division

represent data that can be counted is shown in pictograms, frequency tables, and bar charts

right-angled containing a 90° angle

rotational symmetry a shape has rotational symmetry if you can turn it less than 360 degrees around its centre point to fit exactly onto itself

round to make a number simpler but keep its value close to what it was

rule a set pattern or law that must be followed

S

scale an object that is used to measure weight

scale a system according to which things are measured

scalene triangle a triangle with sides that are three different lengths

sequence a list of numbers in which each number is obtained according to a specific rule

solution the correct answer to a problem

square a 2-D shape with four sides that are the same length and four right angles

subtraction to take away one number from another or find the difference between two numbers

sum the total you get after adding numbers together

symmetry a shape has symmetry if you can draw one or more lines of symmetry (mirror lines) through it; each half on either side of the line will be a reflection of the other

systematic done according to a fixed plan or system

T

table information arranged in rows and columns

temperature how hot or cold something is

ten ten groups of one

tenth one part of something that has been divided equally into ten parts or ten times a hundred or has been made ten times smaller

term number sequences follow a rule that connects each value within them. These values are called terms. Example: when you count 0, 1, 2, 3, 4 … the sequence of numbers follows the rule that the next term is always one more than the previous term.

thousand a hundred times ten

timetable any plan or schedule showing the times at which certain things will happen

total the final number when everything has been counted or calculated

transformation transformation is when you translate, rotate or reflect a shape so that it is in a different position

translation translation is when you move a shape along a straight line without changing the way it looks, for example you can move it up and down, left or right

U

units whole numbers less than 10

units standards of measurement, for example kg or mm

unlikely not a very good chance of happening

V

vertex a corner or a point where the sides of a shape meet to form an angle

vertices plural of vertex

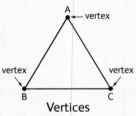

Vertices

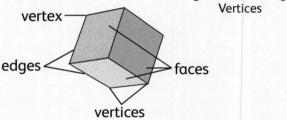

W

weight how heavy something is when you weigh it

whole number a number that does not have fractions or decimals

X

x-axis the horizontal axis of a coordinate grid

Y

y-axis the vertical axis of a coordinate grid

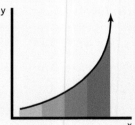

Z

zero having no quantity or number; shown by the symbol 0